OPTIONS TRADING

A guide to invest and make profits with options trading even for beginners, Learn how to make money using risk management, simple steps and strategies on stock trading and investing in the stock market

Ray Aziz

TABLE OF CONTENTS

INTRODUCTION

W hy is it that options are so confused as a minefield of risk and danger? How can you comprehend this and see options as instruments to limit our risks, augment our profits, and SEE WHAT WE'RE DOING simultaneously? This is the importance of Option Easy and this book—how to make complex things basic. Options have gotten surprisingly mainstream, particularly in the U.S. A long way from being restricted exclusively to the organizations and professional money directors, options trading is presently mainstream for "retail" traders from all walks of life.

The idea of options is still, notwithstanding, treated with trepidation and fear in certain quarters. At the point when I initially embark upon genuine trading, a friend told me about what I was getting into, but trading can be as safe as you need it to be. The basic certainty is you have to have a trading plan that works. It needs to keep your risk low and your potential for high reward. You need your arrangement to have simplicity and structure so you can tail it every time. Over the years, my trading plan has gotten logically less difficult. To make it as a trader, it assists with building up the following characteristics—and they can all be developed.

Criteria for Successful Investing

- Patience
- Perseverance
- Knowledge

- Honesty

- Pre-planning

- Discipline

Patience

Making tons of cash in the market is one of the most energizing experiences you can have in your professional life. I've done it in two different ways, making a huge number of gains each time. The first was likely more luck than judgment. The latter was by utilizing aptitudes that took time to develop. Take time to decide on your technique. There comes a time when you feel at one with the markets and trade just whenever the most evident of opportunities stares at you. Whenever you can turn down substandard opportunities with a shrug of the shoulder, you'll realize you've arrived.

In case you're new to all of this, take your time. Consider it along these lines: Would you see yourself as able to do brain surgery after only one instructional exercise? Well, the same applies to trade, and considerably more so for options trading (although same principles apply). Allow yourself to learn. By reading this book, you are doing only that, giving yourself a learning opportunity. If you are already acquainted with stocks, this is the subsequent stage. And just as you needed to get settled with trading stocks from the start, you likewise need to get comfortable with trading options.

Besides, when you are calm enough to trade, you need to be patient to do the trading itself. We've all had the experience of bouncing into a venture too soon even when we were not exactly persuaded it was the proper thing to do. Be patient, take a full breath if you need to, and adhere to your trading plan.

Patience also incorporates choosing a trading technique where time works in your favor and where your drawback is secured. There are a lot of procedures for you to browse in this book, however, you can generally choose to keep things basic. Regardless of which one you pick, consistently hang tight for the right opportunity to present itself. I stick to a few chart patterns to trade, and if they are not appearing, I do not need to trade. Individuals who specialize get the most cash-flow. Along these lines, specialize in terms of what you trade.

Be patient in your disposition for securing wealth. The more patient you are, the happier you will be. This doesn't mean sitting back and sitting idle—that is apathy, not patience. Allow yourself to learn, gain experience, and afterward start to apply what you learn reliably with the goal that you start a process of making money and building riches/wealth.

Perseverance

Keep going. If you believe in something, you need to keep at it until you arrive at your goal. What's more, when you've arrived at your goal, set another target.

Having set out on the objective of turning into a successful trader (whether part-time or full time), you should adhere to it to arrive. Anybody can do it. I've seen it on numerous occasions, where sometimes the most improbable characters become remarkable traders—even those who don't think they can. Practically, give yourself feasible targets to reach in a reasonable time frame. So one week later, you'll be completely acquainted with the four fundamental options risk profiles.

You may just be able to do it tonight. Continue setting the achievable targets (do make them a slight test, however), and along these lines, you will be able to keep up the energy of learning and gaining experience. You will also begin to develop your confidence, reassuring yourself of your ability to comprehend anything you set your mind to. This book will help you in building your confidence.

Knowledge

Having set up the need for patience for both procuring the knowledge and for trading itself, how about we recall that knowledge is attainable now without any difficulty and speed that it is prominently achievable in a sensibly fast time. Apparatuses exist presently to stimulate the trading experience, and there are websites and myriad publications designed to help you with building your knowledge database.

The best knowledge originates from experience. It is all well to say, "Trade mechanically," however not many individuals do. Emotions are part of our being, so instead of disregarding them, it's more useful to work around them. That is what my trading plan is tied in with—staying safe, however still being able to play for the huge successes. The mindset is key.

Recall that learning is experience-based. We all can remember the most extreme teacher at school, isn't that so? You can remember the most entertaining, the most terrifying, the prettiest, the ugliest, and the smelliest, but I will bet you have an issue recollecting anything about the instructors who were somewhere in the middle—the individuals who scarcely had an experiential effect on you in years of being in the same classroom.

The same goes for trading. A great deal of the learning associated with trading is experience-based. Truth be told, the most relevant type of learning about trading is experience-based. It's through the outrageous experience that you discover more about yourself in all sorts of challenges. Most brilliant traders have had horrible encounters but, vitally, have stepped back up to the plate and applied what they've learned much the same as me. I made a ton of cash very quickly, though I was invincible, and afterward instantly gave some of it back once more. Trust me, I didn't feel too great about that, however, I learned. Also, more critically, I applied the lessons.

Thus, permit yourself to get your experience, which is what this book is all about.

Honesty

You must be honest with yourself if you are to develop into a decent investor or trader. At last, your outcomes decide how great you are. Your choices are your responsibility, not anybody else's. Accusing others never makes a difference. If you pull the trigger, then you are the one in charge.

Pre-Planning

You must pre-plan every trade. By this, you must know your

- Breakeven points
- Maximum risk
- Maximum reward

You should also plan:

- Your entrance point
- Your exit point whether to...
- Stop losses or
- Take profit

With options trading, I will in general base any stop loss dependent on the underlying stock.

The fundamental stock is perpetually more liquid than its options, so it makes it simpler to settle on your loss-cutting choice dependent on the cost of the stock, future, or whatever the underlying resource is.

The main bit of pre-planning is simply the decision of the underlying stock because of the outline pattern. At that point, you make the trading plan, which requires...

Discipline — The Key to Success

When you have had the patience to gain the knowledge and apply the standards recently talked about, it's important not to squander everything. You should be disciplined and apply that discipline thoroughly every single time.

This implies:

- You do your pre-planning every time.
- You utilize your experience and that of others.
- You don't deviate from your stated reasonable plan.

Along these lines, you find a way to become more precise. Discipline is essential for trading. Without money management, even the most refined of trading frameworks can't work.

By adhering thoroughly to reasonable money-management standards, you guarantee that your losses are limited and your profits are permitted to run.

You will also make sure that you avoid suicidal risk profiles. I'm regularly stunned at purported specialists teaching option strategies that have horrendous risk profile curves. So we should examine a risk profile and why it is so essential to your prosperity as an options trader.

The Definition of an Option

An option is defined as the "right, not the responsibility, to purchase (or sell) an asset at a fixed cost before a fixed date."

We should examine that definition and check whether we can choose the parts:

- the right, not the responsibility
- to purchase or sell an asset
- at a fixed price
- before a fixed date

These segment parts have significant outcomes on the valuation of an option. Recall that the option itself has a value, which we take a look at after we get done with the definitions.

Before we go ahead and take a look at the manners by which options are esteemed, we should consider the words, "right, not the responsibility."

Chapter 1:
OPTIONS TRADING BASICS

Trading options is a great deal like trading stocks, however, there are significant differences. In contrast to stocks, options come in two kinds (puts and calls) and these options are contracts (as opposed to shares) that give the owner the right to purchase or sell fundamental security like a stock. Like stocks, in any case, options are exchanged on trades and individual dealers can get solicitations to buy and sell through a financier firm.

Options trading isn't new. Indeed, the primal listed options contract made its presentation on the Chicago Board Options Exchange in 1973. While an option today is fundamentally the same as what it was around then, numerous things have changed. The greatest distinction is the size of the market in terms of contracts traded, investors, and several trades. It has developed exponentially and there are more individuals trading options now than ever before.

Investors use options for a wide range of reasons. A call option is an agreement that gives the investor the option to purchase a stock at a set cost for a certain timeframe. A few investors purchase calls when they expect the offer cost to move higher. Others may sell calls when they expect that the cost of stock should move lower or trade flat.

A put option represents the right to sell a security at a pre-decided value (the strike cost) for a predefined timeframe. An investor may purchase a put if they expect that the cost of stock should move lower or as a protective position. A put seller is committed to purchasing the stock at the strike cost through a lapse period.

Calls and puts can be utilized in a bunch of approaches to make distinctive potential rewards and risks situations. Complex strategies like butterflies, straddles, and calendars lie outside the extent of this book, however, regardless of the option contract or the motivation for selling and purchasing, the orders are submitted to a brokerage firm and afterward the transaction happen one of the trades.

Before we dig profound into the universe of options trading, let's take a minute to comprehend why we need options at all. If you are thinking it is simply another approach to bring in money and was made by some extravagant folks in suits working in Wall Street, well, you are incorrect. The options world originates before the modern stock trades by an enormous margin.

While some praise the Samurai for giving us the establishment on which options contracts were based, some recognize the Greeks for giving us a thought on the most proficient method to how to speculate on a commodity, for this situation, the harvest of olives. In the two cases, people were attempting to figure the cost of a food thing and trade accordingly, sometime before the advanced world put in various guidelines and set up trades.
Because of this, let us try to address the primary question in your mind.

OPTIONS TRADING GUIDE FOR BEGINNERS

<u>What is options trading?</u>

How about we take a very simple example to comprehend options trading. Consider that you are purchasing a stock for Rs. 3000. However, the broker informs you regarding an energizing offer, that you can get it now for Rs. 3000 or you can give a token of Rs. 30 and reserve the right to purchase it at Rs. 3000 following a month, even if the stock increments in value at that time. But, that amount is non-refundable!

You understand that there is a high possibility that the stock would cross Rs. 3030 and in this way, you can breakeven at least. Since you need to pay just Rs. 30 now, the remaining amount can be utilized somewhere else for a month. You sit tight for a month and afterward take a look at the stock cost.

Presently, contingent upon the stock price, you have the choice to purchase the stock from the broker or not. This is an over-simplification, however, this is options trading in a gist. In the universe of trading, options are instruments that belong to the subsidiary's family, which implies its cost is gotten from something else, generally stocks. The cost of an option is intrinsically connected to the cost of the underlying stock.

Options are contingent subordinate agreements that permit purchasers of the agreements (option holders) to purchase or sell a security at a picked cost. Option purchasers are charged a sum called a "premium" by the sellers for such a right. Should market price be disparaging for option holders, they will let the option expire worthlessly, thus ensuring the losses are not greater than the premium.

Interestingly, option sellers assume more serious risk than the option purchasers, which is the reason they demand this premium.

Options are divided into "put" and "call" options. With a call option, the purchaser of the contract buys the option to purchase the fundamental asset later on at a foreordained price, called strike price or exercise price. With a put option, the purchaser gets the option to sell the fundamental asset in the future at the predetermined price.

Why Trade Options Instead Of a Direct Asset?

The Chicago Board of Options Exchange (CBOE) is the greatest such trade in the world, offering options on a wide range of indexes, ETF's, and single stocks. Traders can develop option strategies ranging from buying or offering a single option to extremely complex ones that include diverse concurrent option positions.

Below are rudimentary option techniques for beginners.

Buying Calls (Long Call)

This is the preferred technique for traders who:

- Are "bullish" or confident on a specific stock, index or ETF and want to confine risk
- Want to use influence to take advantage of rising costs

Options are leveraged instruments, i.e., they permit traders to enhance the advantage by risking littler sums than would somehow be required if trading the underlying asset itself. A standard option contract on a stock controls a hundred shares of fundamental security.

Assume a broker needs to put $5,000 in Apple (AAPL), trading around $165 per share. With this sum, the person in question can buy 30 offers for $4,950. Assume then that the cost of the stock increments by 10% to $181.50 throughout the following month. Ignoring any transaction fees, commission, or brokerage, the dealer's portfolio will increase to $5,445, leaving the dealer with a net return of $495, or 10 percent on the investment.

Assume a call option on the stock with a strike cost of $165 that expires about a month from now costs $550 per contract or $5.50 per share. Given the dealer's investment budget, the individual in question can purchase nine options for an expense of $4,950. Since the option contract controls 100 shares, the dealer is adequately arranging 900 shares. If the stock cost expands 10% to $181.50 at lapse, the option will terminate in the money and be worth $16.50 per share ($181.50-$165 strike), or $14,850 on 900 shares. That is a net dollar return of $9,990, or 200% on the capital contributed, a lot bigger return contrasted with trading the fundamental asset straightforwardly.

Reward/Risk: The broker's potential loss from a long call is restricted to the premium paid. Potential profit is boundless, as the option payoff will increment alongside the fundamental asset cost until lapse, and there is hypothetically no restriction to how high it can go.

Long Put (Buying Put)

This is the favored technique for traders who:

- Are bearish on a specific stock, index or ETF, however, want to face less challenge than with a short-selling procedure
- Want to use leverage to take advantage of falling costs

A put option works the specific inverse way a call option does, with the put option picking up an incentive as the cost of the basic reductions. While short-selling additionally permits a broker to profit from falling costs, the risk with a short position is boundless, as there is hypothetically no restriction on how high a cost can rise. With a put option, if the basic increments past the option's strike value, the option will simply expire worthlessly.

Risk/Reward: Possible loss is limited to the premium paid for the options.

The maximum profit from the position is topped since the basic cost can't drop below zero, however, similarly as with a long call option, the put option uses the dealer's return.

Covered Call

This is the favored position for traders who:

- Expect slight increase or no change in the underlying's cost
- Are willing to constrain upside potential in return for some downside protection

A covered call strategy involves purchasing 100 shares of the underlying resource and selling a call option against those shares. At the point when the broker sells the call, he gathers the option's premium, along these lines bringing down the cost premise on the offers and giving some downside protection. Consequently, by selling the option, the broker is consenting to sell shares of the underlying at the option's strike cost, in this manner topping the dealer's upside potential.

Suppose a dealer buys 1,000 shares of (BP) at 44USD per share and at the same time writes 10 call options (1 agreement/contract for every 100 offers) with a strike cost of 46USD expiring in 1 month, to a detriment of 0.25USD per share, or 25USD per contract and 250USD total for the 10 agreements/contract. The 0.25USD premium reduces the price premise on the shares to 43.75USD, so any drop in the underlying down to this point will be balanced by the premium gotten from the option position, along these lines offering restricted downside protection.

If the share value transcends $46 before the lapse, the short call option will be exercised (or "summoned"), which means the trader should deliver the stock at the option's strike cost. For this situation, the broker will make a profit of $2.25 per share ($46 strike cost - $43.75 cost premise).

In any case, this model infers the broker doesn't expect BP to move above $46 or fundamentally beneath $44 throughout the following month. As long as the shares don't rise above $46 and get summoned before the options terminate, the dealer will keep the premium clear and free and can keep selling calls against the shares if he chooses.

Reward/Risk: If the share price transcends the strike cost before the lapse, the short call option can be practiced and the dealer should deliver shares of underling at the option's strike price, even if it is beneath the market price. As a byproduct of this risk, a covered call strategy gives confined drawback protection as premium got when selling the call option.

Protective Put

This is the favored strategy for traders who:

• Own the basic asset and need drawback protection.

A Protective put is a long put, similar to the strategy we talked about above; however, the objective, as the name suggests, is downside protection as opposed to trying to profit from a downside move. If a broker owns shares that the person is bullish on over the long haul but wants to protect against a decrease in the short run, they may buy a protective put.

If the price of the basic increments and is over the put's strike price at development, the option lapses worthless and the dealer loses the premium but at the same time has the benefit of the increased basic price. Then again, if the underlying price diminishes, the trader's portfolio position loses value, however, this loss is to a great extent covered by the gain from the put option position. Subsequently, the position can adequately be thought of as a protection technique.

The broker can set the strike price underneath the present price to lessen premium payment to the detriment of diminishing downside protection. This can be thought of as deductible protection. Assume, for instance, that an investor purchases 1,000 shares of Coca-Cola (KO) for $44 and needs to protect the investment from unfavorable price developments throughout the next two months.

Reward/Risk: If the cost of the basic remains the equivalent or rises, the potential misfortune will be constrained to the option premium, which is paid as protection. If the cost of the underlying falls, the loss in the capital will be balanced by an expansion in the option's cost and is restricted to the distinction between the underlying strike price and stock price in addition to the premium paid for the option. In the above model, at the strike price of 4USD0, the loss is limited to 4.20USD per share (44USD – 40USD + 0.20USD).

Other Options Strategies

These strategies might be somewhat more perplexing than basically purchasing puts or calls, yet they are intended to assist you with bettering deal with the risk of options trading:

- **Buy-write strategy or Covered call strategy:** Stocks are purchased, and the financial specialist sells call options on the same stock. The number of shares you purchased ought to be identical to the number of call options contracts you sold.

- **Married Put Strategy:** After buying a stock, the dealer buys put options for an equivalent number of shares. The married put works like an insurance approach against momentary losses call options with a specific strike price. At the same time, you will sell the same number of call options at a higher strike cost.
- **Protective Collar Strategy:** A dealer buys an out-of-the-money put option, while all the while working an out-of-the-money call option for a comparable stock.
- **Long Straddle Strategy:** The dealer buys a put option and a call option simultaneously. The two options ought to have the same strike price and the same expiration.
- **Long Strangle Strategy:** Investor buys an out-of-the-money put option and a call option simultaneously. They have a similar lapse date, but, they have differing strike prices. The put strike price should be lower than the call strike price.

Options offer alternative techniques for investors to profit from trading protections. There's an assortment of strategies involving underlying assets, various combinations of options, and other derivatives. Fundamental methodologies for beginners incorporate purchasing calls, purchasing puts, selling covered calls, and purchasing protective puts. There are advantages to trading options as opposed to underlying assets, for example, leveraged returns and downside protection, but there are also disadvantages like the necessity for forthright premium payment. Picking a broker is the first step to trading options.

A formal definition is given below:

A stock option is an agreement between two people or parties wherein the stock option purchaser (holder) buys the right (but not the responsibility) to purchase/sell shares of a basic stock at a fixed price from/to the option seller (writer) within a given period.

OPTIONS TRADING VS. STOCK TRADING

There must be uncertainty in your mind that why do we have options trading if it is simply another method of trading. Indeed, here are a couple of points which make it unique to trading stocks;

- The Options contract has a lapse date, unlike stocks. The termination can vary from weeks, months to years contingent on the guidelines and the sort of Options that you are practicing. Stocks, on the other hand, don't have a termination or expiration date.
- Unlike Stocks, Options get their value from something different and that is the reason they fall under the derivatives class.
- Options are not distinct by numbers like Stocks.
- Options proprietors/owners have no right (dividend or voting) in an organization, unlike Stock owners.

Some people often find the Option's concept hard to comprehend, however, they have just tailed it in their other transactions, for example, mortgages or car insurance.

OPTIONS TERMINOLOGIES

Premium

Since the Options themselves do not have fundamental value, the Options premium is the price that you need to pay to buy an Option. The premium is dictated by different variables including the underlying stock value, unpredictability in the market, and the days until the Option's expiration. In options trading, picking the premium is one of the most significant components.

Strike Price

This is the price at which the underlying stocks can be sold or purchased according to the agreement/contract. In options trading, the Strike Price for a Call Option shows the cost at which the Stock can be purchased (on or before its termination date) and for Put Options trading it alludes to the cost at which the seller can practice its entitlement to sell the underlying stocks (on or before its termination)

Underlying Asset

In options trading, the fundamental asset can be stocks, index, commodity, futures, or currency. The price of Options is gotten from its underlying asset. The Option of stock gives the option to purchase or sell the stock at a particular cost and date to the holder. Thus, it is all about the fundamental stocks or assets when it comes to Stock in Options Trading.

Expiration Date

In options trading, every single stock option has an expiration date. The expiration date is the last date on which the Options holder can practice the right to purchase or sell the Options that are in holding. In Options Trading, the expiration of Options can vary from weeks to months to years contingent upon the regulations and the market.

Options Style

There are two significant sorts of Options that are practiced in most of the options trading markets.

- American Options which can be practiced anytime before its lapse date
- European Options must be practiced upon the arrival of its lapse or expiration.

Moneyness (ITM, OTM & ATM)

It is imperative to comprehend the Options Moneyness before you begin trading in Stock Options. A great deal of options trading methodologies is played around the Moneyness of an Option.

It essentially defines the connection between the strike cost of an Option and the present cost of the underlying Stocks. We will look at each term in detail below.

When is an Option in-the-money?

- Put Option - when the underlying strike price is higher than the stock price.
- Call Option – when the underlying strike price is lower than the stock price.

When is an Option out-of-the-money?

- Call Option – when the underlying strike price is higher than the stock price.
- Put Option – this is when the underlying strike price is lower than the stock price.

<u>When is an Option at-the-money?</u>

•When the underlying stock cost is equivalent to the strike cost

Take a break here to consider over the various terms as we will discover it incredibly helpful later when we go through the kinds of options just as a couple of options trading techniques.

TYPE OF OPTIONS

In a genuine sense, there are just two types of Options i.e Put and Call Options. We will understand them in more detail.

To Call or Put

A Call Option is an option to purchase an underlying Stock on or before its termination date. At the hour of purchasing a Call Option, you pay a specific amount of premium to the seller which awards you the right (but not the responsibility) to purchase the underlying stock at a predetermined value (strike price).

Buying a call option implies that you are bullish about the market and trusting that the cost of the underlying stock may go up. To make a profit, the cost of the stock ought to go higher than the strike cost plus the premium of the call option that you have bought before or at the hour of its lapse.

Excitingly, a Put Option is an option to sell an underlying Stock on or before its termination date. Buying a Put Option implies that you are bearish about the market and trusting that the cost of the underlying stock may go down. With the end goal for you to make a profit, the cost of the stock ought to go down from the strike price in addition to the premium of the Put Option that you have bought previously or at the hour of its termination.

Thusly, both Call and Put option purchaser's loss is constrained to the premium paid, however, profit is boundless. The above clarifications were from the purchaser's perspective. We will now comprehend the put-call options from the seller's perspective, which is options writers. The Put option sellers, as an end-result of the premium charged, are committed to purchasing the basic asset at the strike price. In like manner, the Call option seller, as a final product of the premium charged, is focused on selling the fundamental asset at the strike price.

Is there an approach to envision the potential profit/loss of an option purchaser or seller? In reality, there is. An option payoff is a graphical portrayal of the Net Profit/Loss made by the option purchasers and sellers.

Before we go through the charts, how about we comprehend what the four terms mean. As we realize that going short means selling and going long means purchasing the asset, a similar rule applies to options.

- Short call - Here we bet that the costs will fall and henceforth, a short call implies you are selling calls.
- Short put - Here the short put implies we are selling a put option.
- Long put - Here we are purchasing a put option.
- Long call - it implies that we are purchasing a call option since we are hopeful about the underlying asset's share cost.

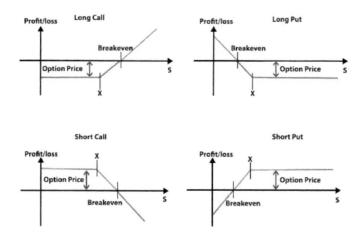

where

S = Underlying Price

X = Strike Price

The breakeven point is that point where you make no loss or no profit.

The long call holder makes a profit equivalent to the stock cost at termination less strike price less premium if the option is in the money. Call option holder makes a loss equivalent to the amount of premium if the option lapses out of money and the writer of the option makes a flat profit equivalent to the option premium.

So also, for the put option purchaser, profit is made when the option is in the money and is equivalent to the strike value less the stock cost at lapse less premium. Also, the put writer makes a profit equivalent to the premium for the option.

OK, until now we have been going through a ton of hypotheses. We should shift gears for a moment and come to reality. What do options look like? All things considered, let's find out.

What does an options trading quote comprise of?

If you somehow managed to search for an option quote on Apple stock, it would look something like this:

OPTIONS

All ▾   Calls and Puts ▾   08/30/2019 ▾

Calls	Last	Change	Bid	Ask	Volume	OpenInt	Strike	Puts	Last	Change	Bid	Ask	Volume	OpenInt
O:AAPL 19H130.00D30			66.95	67.50	0	0	130.00	O:AAPL 19T130.00D30			0.02	0.07	0	0
O:AAPL 19H135.00D30			61.95	62.50	0	0	135.00	O:AAPL 19T135.00D30			0.06	0.10	0	0
O:AAPL 19H140.00D30			56.90	57.60	0	0	140.00	O:AAPL 19T140.00D30			0.10	0.14	0	0
O:AAPL 19H145.00D30			52.00	52.55	0	0	145.00	O:AAPL 19T145.00D30			0.16	0.19	0	0
O:AAPL 19H150.00D30	57.70	0.00	47.05	47.55	0	1	150.00	O:AAPL 19T150.00D30	0.33	+0.12	0.23	0.28	0	214
O:AAPL 19H152.50D30			44.55	45.05	0	0	152.50	O:AAPL 19T152.50D30			0.28	0.32	0	0
O:AAPL 19H155.00D50			42.10	42.60	0	0	155.00	O:AAPL 19T155.00D30	0.33	-0.22	0.34	0.36	15	151
O:AAPL 19H157.50D30			39.60	40.10	0	0	157.50	O:AAPL 19T157.50D30			0.39	0.43	0	0
O:AAPL 19H160.00D30	35.20	0.00	37.15	37.65	0	2	160.00	O:AAPL 19T160.00D30	0.42	-0.33	0.47	0.50	3,767	4,924
O:AAPL 19H162.50D30			34.70	35.20	0	0	162.50	O:AAPL 19T162.50D30			0.55	0.59	0	0
O:AAPL 19H165.00D30			32.30	32.75	0	0	165.00	O:AAPL 19T165.00D30	0.64	-0.46	0.63	0.68	16	253
O:AAPL 19H167.50D30			29.85	30.35	0	0	167.50	O:AAPL 19T167.50D30			0.75	0.81	0	0
O:AAPL 19H170.00D30	34.00	-15.50	27.50	27.95	0	153	170.00	O:AAPL 19T170.00D30	0.89	-0.53	0.89	0.96	3	411
O:AAPL 19H172.50D30	23.80	-0.45	25.15	25.88	0	17	172.50	O:AAPL 19T172.50D30	1.45	-0.33	1.06	1.12	1	499
O:AAPL 19H175.00D30	28.85	-4.72	22.85	23.25	0	113	175.00	O:AAPL 19T175.00D30	1.23	-0.81	1.28	1.35	3	338
O:AAPL 19H177.50D30	20.87	+2.53	20.70	21.05	1	118	177.50	O:AAPL 19T177.50D30	1.50	-0.90	1.53	1.60	54	110
O:AAPL 19H180.00D30	16.26	-7.39	18.50	18.85	0	219	180.00	O:AAPL 19T180.00D30	1.83	-1.06	1.84	1.91	42	1,268
O:AAPL 19H182.50D30	13.85	-7.55	16.40	16.53	0	244	182.50	O:AAPL 19T182.50D30	2.09	-1.12	2.22	2.31	3	247
O:AAPL 19H185.00D30	14.55	+2.35	14.40	14.55	10	160	185.00	O:AAPL 19T185.00D30	2.67	-1.38	2.69	2.77	58	1,053
O:AAPL 19H187.50D30	12.65	+2.18	12.45	12.60	6	106	187.50	O:AAPL 19T187.50D30	3.23	-1.56	3.25	3.35	113	693
O:AAPL 19H190.00D30	11.00	+2.31	10.65	10.80	33	440	190.00	O:AAPL 19T190.00D30	3.84	-1.93	3.96	4.05	432	1,973
O:AAPL 19H192.50D30	9.10	+1.70	8.95	9.10	10	277	192.50	O:AAPL 19T192.50D30	4.68	-2.11	4.75	4.90	174	906
O:AAPL 19H195.00D30	7.60	+1.80	7.40	7.55	38	604	195.00	O:AAPL 19T195.00D30	5.80	-2.20	5.70	5.89	29	6,922
O:AAPL 19H197.50D30	6.05	+1.30	6.06	6.15	26	307	197.50	O:AAPL 19T197.50D30	6.65	-2.55	6.75	6.90	11	320
O:AAPL 19H200.00D30	4.90	+1.20	4.80	4.95	505	660	200.00	O:AAPL 19T200.00D30	7.91	-2.87	8.05	8.20	4	1,357
O:AAPL 19H202.50D30	3.85	+0.95	3.75	3.85	15	354	202.50	O:AAPL 19T202.50D30	9.31	-3.18	9.50	9.65	11	300
O:AAPL 19H205.00D30	2.90	+0.65	2.88	2.95	170	1,036	205.00	O:AAPL 19T205.00D30	10.65	-3.75	11.13	11.30	2	641
O:AAPL 19H207.50D30	2.25	+0.55	2.16	2.22	124	666	207.50	O:AAPL 19T207.50D30	13.05	-2.95	12.90	13.05	14	741
O:AAPL 19H210.00D30	1.60	+0.30	1.59	1.66	92	1,799	210.00	O:AAPL 19T210.00D30	14.78	-1.56	14.80	15.05	12	1,156
O:AAPL 19H212.50D30	1.20	+0.27	1.12	1.21	4	1,331	212.50	O:AAPL 19T212.50D30	16.81	-3.38	16.75	17.10	5	549
O:AAPL 19H215.00D30	0.83	+0.16	0.81	0.89	17	1,890	215.00	O:AAPL 19T215.00D30	19.25	-4.70	18.95	19.35	1	775
O:AAPL 19H217.50D30	0.61	+0.13	0.58	0.62	1	1,455	217.50	O:AAPL 19T217.50D30	21.20	-3.90	21.10	21.85	10	227

When this was recorded, the stock price of Apple Inc. was $196. Now let's take one line from the list and break it down further.

Eg.

Calls	Last	Change	Bid	Ask	Volume	OpenInt	Strike	Puts	Last	Change	Bid	Ask	Volume	OpenInt
O:AAPL 19H170.00D30	34.00	-15.50	27.50	27.95	0	153	170.00	O:AAPL 19T170.00D30	0.89	-0.53	0.89	0.96	3	411

In a typical options chain, you will have a rundown of put and call options with various strike prices and corresponding premiums. The put options details are on the right and the call option details are on the left with the strike price in the middle.

- The option number and the symbol is the first column.
- The "last" column connotes the sum at which the last time the option was purchased.
- "Change" shows the fluctuation between the last two trades of the said options.
- "Bid" column designates the offer submitted for the option.
- "Ask" shows the asking cost sought by the option seller.
- "Volume" shows the number of options traded. Here the volume is 0.
- "Open Interest" shows the number of options that can be purchased at that strike price.

The columns are the equivalent for the put options also. Sometimes, the data provider means whether the option is in the money, at the money or out of money too. We need a guide to truly help our comprehension of options trading. Hence, we should go through one at this point.

Options Trading Example

We will go through 2 cases to better comprehend the put and call options.

For the good of simplicity, let us assume the following:

- Cost of Stock when the options are written: $100

- Premium: $5

- Expiration date: one month after the option is purchased

Case one:

The present strike price: $120. Price of stock: $110.

Type of Option	Owner	Moneyness	Result
Call	Options buyer	Out of the money	If the options buyer proceeds to buy the stock from the options seller, the total amount given by the buyer of a stock is: ($120 +$5 = $125) Since it is better to buy the stock directly, the buyer would not exercise the option.
Call	Options writer	Out of the money	Since the options buyer does not exercise the option, the options writer makes a profit which is equal to the premium.
Put	Option buyer	In the money	Since the options buyer can sell the stock at $120 and thus, the total amount gained in the process ($120 - $5) = $115, which is higher than the stock at $110, the options buyer will exercise the put option.
Put	Option writer	In the money	As the put option is exercised, The options writer reports a loss of ($120 - $110 - $5) = $5

Case two:

The current strike price: $110. Price of stock: $120.

Type of Option	Owner	Moneyness	Result
Call	Options buyer	In the money	If the option buyer proceeds to buy the stock from the option seller, the total amount given by the buyer of stock is: ($110 + $5 = $115) Since the current price of the stock is $120, the buyer will make a profit of $5 when they sell the stock in the market. Thus, the option will be exercised.
Call	Options writer	In the money	Since the option buyer exercises the option, the option writer will technically book a loss of ($120 -$110 - $5 = $5).
Put	Option buyer	Out of the money	Technically, the put option buyer could sell the stock in the market for $120 rather than sell it to the option writer at the agreed-upon strike price of $110. Thus, the option buyer would let the option expire and register a loss of $5 which is equal to the premium paid.
Put	Options writer	Out of the money	As the put option is not exercised, The option writer reports a profit of $5 which is equal to the premium paid.

Since we have gone through the detailed situation of every option, we should join a couple of options together. Let's comprehend a significant concept which numerous experts use in options trading.

What is Put-Call Parity In Python?

Put-call parity is an idea that any individual who is keen on options trading needs to comprehend. By gaining a comprehension of put-call parity you can comprehend how the estimation of a call option, put option and the stock are connected. This empowers you to make other synthetic position utilizing different option and stock mix.

The principle of put-call parity

The rule of Put-call parity describes the association between the cost of a European Call option and European Put option, both having the equal expiration date, strike price, and underlying asset. If there is a deviation from put-call parity, at that point it would result in an exchange opportunity. Traders would make the most of this chance to make riskless profits till the time the put-call equality is set up once more.

The put-call parity rule can be utilized to approve an option estimating model. If the option costs as computed by the model disregard the put-call parity rule, such a model can be viewed as incorrect.

Understanding Put-Call Parity

To comprehend put-call parity, consider a portfolio "A" encompassing call option and money. The amount of money held equals the call strike cost. Consider another portfolio "B" including a put option and the underlying asset.

Required Conditions For Put-call Parity

For put-call parity to hold, the accompanying conditions ought to be met. In any case, in reality, they barely remain true and the put-call parity equation may require a few alterations in like manner.

- The underlying stock does not deliver any dividend during the life of the European options
- There are no tax duties
- There are no exchange costs
- Shorting is permitted and there are no borrow charges

Consequently, put-call parity will hold in a frictionless market with the underlying stock delivering no dividends.

Arbitrage Opportunity

In options trading, when the put-call parity rule gets disregarded, traders will attempt to make the most of the arbitrage opportunity. An arbitrage trader will go long on the disparaged portfolio and short the overstated portfolio to make a risk free profit.

The most effective method to make the most of arbitrage opportunity

Let us consider a model with certain numbers to perceive how trade can make the most of arbitrage opportunities. How about we assume that the spot cost of a stock is $31, the risk-free interest rate is 10% yearly, the premium on 3-month European put and call are $2.25 and $3 respectively and the exercise cost is $30.

For this situation, the value of portfolio A will be,

C+Xe-rT = 3+30e-0.1 * 3/12 = $32.26

The value of portfolio B will be,

P + So = 2.25 + 31 = $33.25

Portfolio B is exaggerated and consequently, an arbitrageur can earn by going short on portfolio B and long on the portfolio. The accompanying steps can be followed to earn arbitrage profits.

- Short the stock. This will produce a cash inflow of $31.
- Short the put option. This will produce a cash inflow of $2.25.
- Purchase the call option. This will produce a cash outflow of $3.
- Total cash inflow is - 3 + 2.25 + 31 = $30.25.
- Invest $30.25 in a zero-coupon bond with three months of development with a yield of 10% yearly.

Come back from the zero coupon bond following 3 months will be 30.25e 0.1 * 3/12 = $31.02.

If the stock price at maturity is over 30USD, the call option will be practiced and if the stock price is lesser than 30USD, the put option will be practiced. In the two circumstances, the arbitrageur will buy one stock at 30USD.

This stock will be utilized to cover the short.

Total profit from the arbitrage = $31.02 - $30 = $1.02

Why is Options Trading alluring?

Options are alluring instruments to trade as a result of the higher yields. An option gives the privilege to the holder to accomplish something, with the 'option' of not to practice that right. Along these lines, the holder can confine his losses and increase his profits.

While the facts show that one option contract is for hundred shares, it is accordingly less risky to pay the premium and not risk the aggregate sum which would need to be utilized if we had purchased the shares instead. In this way, your risk exposure is greatly reduced. However, as a general rule, options trading is unpredictable and that is because options pricing models are very complex and mathematical.

So, how do you evaluate if the option is extremely worth purchasing?

The key to effective options trading strategies includes understanding and executing options pricing models. In this segment, we will get a short comprehension of Greeks in options that will help in making and understanding the pricing models.

OPTIONS PRICING

Options Pricing depends on two sorts of values

Intrinsic Value of an option

Remember the moneyness concept that went through a couple of segments back. When the call option stock price is over the strike price or when put option stock price is less than the strike value, the option is said to be "In-The-Money (ITM)", that is, it has an inherent value. Then again, "Out of the money (OTM)" options have no intrinsic value. For "Out Of The Money" OTM call options, the stock price is less than the strike price and for OTM put options; stock price is over the strike price. The price of these options comprises completely of time value.

Time Value of an option

If you take away the amount of intrinsic value from the value of an option, you are left with the time value. It depends on the expiration time. We realize what is characteristic and the time estimation of an option. How do we realize that one option is better than the other, and how to quantify the adjustments in option pricing. How about we take the help of the greeks at this point.

Options Greeks

Greeks are the risk measures related to different situations in options trading. The basic ones are gamma, delta, vega, and theta. With the adjustment in volatility or prices of the basic stock, you have to know how your options pricing would be influenced. Greeks in options assist us with understanding how the different factors, for example, time to expiry, prices, volatility affect the options pricing.

Delta measures the affectability of an option's price to an adjustment in the price of the basic stock. Delta is that options greek which reveals to you how much money a stock option will drop or rise in worth with a $1 drop or rise in the underlying stock. Delta is reliant on basic price, volatility, and time to expiry. While the equation for figuring delta is based on the Black-Scholes option-pricing model, we can write it as,

Delta = [Expected change in Premium] / [Change in the price of the underlying stock]

Python Library - Mibian

What is Mibian?

Mibian is an options pricing/estimating Python library executing the Black-Scholes alongside a couple different models for European options on stocks and currencies. We are going to take a look at the Black-Scholes part of this library. Mibian is good with python 2.7 and 3.x. This library requires scipy to work appropriately.

How to utilize Mibian for BS Model?

The function which constructs the Black-Scholes model in this library is the BS() function. Below is the syntax for this function;

BS ([underlyingPrice, strikePrice, interestRate, daysToExpiration], volatility=x, callPrice=y, putPrice=z)

The primary input is a rundown containing the price, interest rate, strike price, and days to expiration. This rundown must be indicated each time the function is being called. Next, we input the volatility, on the off chance that we are keen on processing the price of the option greeks and options. The BS function will just contain two contentions.

If we are keen on computing the implied volatility, we won't input the volatility, but rather will enter either the put price or the call price. If we are keen on figuring the put-call parity, we will enter both the call price and put price after the rundown. The value returned would be:

(call price + price of the bond worth the strike price at maturity) - (put price + underlying asset price)

Derman Kani Model

The Derman Kani model was created to beat the long-standing issue with the Black Scholes model, which is the volatility grin. One of the fundamental assumptions of the Black Scholes model is that the underlying follows an arbitrary walk with steady volatility. Notwithstanding, on ascertaining the inferred volatility for various strikes, it is seen that the volatility curve is certainly not a constant straight line as we would expect, but rather has the state of a smile. The curve of implied volatility against the strike price is known as the volatility smile.

If the Black Scholes model is right, it would imply that the underlying follows a lognormal dispersion and the inferred volatility curve would have been level, but a volatility smile shows that traders are certainly attributing an exceptional non-lognormal distribution to the underlying. This non-lognormal dispersion can be credited to the underlying following a modified random walk, as in the volatility isn't consistent and changes with both stock time and price. To accurately value the options, we would need to know the specific type of the modified random walk.

The Derman Kani model tells the best way to take the inferred volatilities as contributions to deduce the type of the underlying's random walk. More precisely a unique binomial tree is separated from the smile comparing to the random walk of the underlying, this tree is known as the implied tree. This tree can be utilized to esteem different subsidiaries whose costs are not promptly accessible from the market - for instance, it tends to be utilized in standard, but American options, exotic options, and illiquid European options.

What is the Heston model?

Steven Heston provided a closed organized solution for the price of a European call option on an asset with stochastic volatility. This model was additionally developed to consider the volatility smile, which couldn't be clarified utilizing the Black Scholes model.

The fundamental supposition of the Heston model is that volatility is an arbitrary variable. Hence there are two arbitrary factors, one for the volatility and the other for underlying. For the most part, when the variance of the underlying has been made stochastic, closed structured solutions will not exist anymore.

In any case, this is a significant advantage of the Heston model, that shut structure arrangements do exist for European plain vanilla options. This component additionally makes adjustments to the model feasible.

Chapter 2:
CHOOSING A BROKER

How to pick a broker for Options Trading?

B efore opening an options trading account with a broker, how about we go over a couple of points to consider when we pick a broker.

- Understand your point when you track the options trading waters, regardless of whether it is a way of hedging risk, as a theoretical instrument, for income generation.
- Does the merchant or broker give option assessment devices of their own? It is always valuable to have access to an overabundance of apparatuses when you are choosing the right option.
- Enquire the commission charged by a broker and the transaction costs as this will eat into your investment profits.
- Some brokers offer access to inquire about materials in different areas of the stock market. You can generally check with the broker about access to investigate as well as subscription and so forth.
- Check the installment options given by the broker to ensure it is well-suited with your convenience.

Searching for the right broker

When the necessary background research is done, you can pick the right broker according to your need and comfort. In the worldwide market, a rundown of the top brokers is given underneath:

Rundown of Top International Brokers (Options Trading)

The rundown of top international options brokers is given underneath:

- E-trade ($0.65 per options contract)
- TD Ameritrade ($0.65 fee per contract)
- Ally Invest ($0.5 per contract traded)
- Schwab Brokerage ($0.65 per options contract)
- Interactive Brokers (starts at $0.25 per options contract)

List of Top Indian Brokers (Options Trading)

The list of top Indian Options Brokers is given below:

- ICICI Direct
- Axis Direct
- HDFC Securities
- ShareKhan
- Zerodha
- Kotak Securities
- Angel Broking

Amazing! Presently we take a look at certain options trading strategies that can be utilized in reality.

TIPS FOR PICKING AN OPTIONS BROKER

However, if you choose your options broker carefully, you'll quickly master how to coordinate research, track positions, and place trade.

Here's our proposal on picking a broker that offers the account features and the service that best serves your options trading requirements.

1. <u>Search for a free education</u>

In case you're new to options trading or need to extend your trading strategies, finding a dealer that has resources for educating clients is an absolute necessity. That training can come in numerous structures, including:

- Online options trading courses.
- Live or recorded online courses.
- One-on-one guidance by phone or online.
- A face-to-face meeting with a bigger dealer that has branches across the nation.

It's a smart thought to spend some time in study-driver mode and absorb as much training and advice as possible. If an agent or a broker offers a recreated type of its options trading platform, test-drive the methodology with a paper trading account before risking money.

2. <u>Put your broker's customer service to the test</u>

Dependable customer service should be a high priority, especially for newer options traders. It's likewise significant for the individuals who are conducting complex trades or switching brokers they may need help with.

Consider what sort of contact you prefer. Email? Live online chat? Telephone support? Does the specialist/broker have a committed trading work area accessible if the need arises? What hours is it staffed? Is technical support available all day, every day, or just weekdays? Shouldn't something is said about delegates who can respond to inquiries regarding your account?

Even before you apply for an account, reach out and pose a few inquiries to check whether the appropriate responses and reaction time are palatable.

3. Make sure the trading platform is simple to utilize

Options trading platforms come in different shapes and sizes. They can be web-or programming based, work area or online just, have separate platforms for fundamental and propelled trading, offer full or incomplete mobile functionality or a combination of the abovementioned.

Visit a broker's site and search for a guided tour through its tools and platform. Video and screenshots instructional exercises are pleasant, but evaluating a dealer's simulated trading platform, f it has one, will give you the best feeling of whether the broker is a solid match.

A few interesting points:

- Is the platform structure easy to use or do you need to hunt and peck to discover what you need?
- How simple is it to place a trade?
- Can the platform do the things you need, such as making alerts dependent on explicit models or letting you fill out an exchange ticket advance to submit later?
- Will you need mobile access to the full set-up of service when you are on the go, or will a pared-down rendition of the platform do the trick?
- How solid is the site, and how rapidly are orders executed? This is a high priority if your strategy includes rapidly entering and leaving positions.
- Does the broker charge a month to month or yearly platform fee? Assuming this is the case, are there approaches to get the expense waived, for example,

40

conducting a certain number of trades or keeping a minimum account balance during a particular period?

4. Evaluate the depth, breadth, and cost of tools and data

Research and Data are an options broker's backbone. Some of the nuts and bolts to search for:

- Frequently updated statements feed.
- Basic diagramming to help pick your exit and entry points
- The ability to dissect a trade's potential rewards and risks (maximum downside and maximum upside).
- Screening devices.

Those wandering into further developed trading strategies may require further expository and trade modeling instruments, for example, customizable screeners; the ability to construct, test, track and back-test trading techniques; and real-time market information from numerous providers.

Verify whether the fancy stuff costs more. For instance, most brokers give free deferred quotes, lagging twenty minutes behind market information, however, charge an expense for an ongoing feed. Likewise, some master level instruments might be available just to clients who meet month to month or account balance or quarterly trading activity.

5. Do not weigh the cost of commissions too heavily

There is a reason commission costs are lower on our rundown. Price isn't all that matters, and it's not as significant as other things we've covered. However, since commissions give a suitable side by side correlation, they often are the main things people see when choosing an options broker.

A couple of things to think about how much brokers charge to trade options:

- The two segments of an options trading commission are the base rate — basically equivalent to the thing as the trading commission that financial specialists pay when they purchase a stock — and the per-contract fee. Commissions have been reduced recently; various brokers directly offer free commissions. Contract costs are between 15 cents to 1.25USD or more.

- Some brokers pack the trading commission and the per-contract expense into a solitary flat charge.
- Some brokers additionally offer limited commissions dependent on trading recurrence, average, or volume account balance. The meaning of "active trader" or "high volume" varies by the brokerage.

In case you're new to options trading or utilize the strategy just sparingly you will well-served by picking either a specialist that offers a solitary level rate to exchange or one that charges no commission (you likely won't have the option to avoid the per-contract expense). In case you're a more active dealer, you should audit your trading rhythm to check whether a layered pricing plan would save you cash.

CHOOSING AN ONLINE OPTIONS BROKER

Of the considerable number of choices you make before really beginning to trade options, the decision of which online options specialist to utilize is without a doubt one of the more significant ones. Such a choice isn't irreversible because you can generally utilize an alternate specialist if the first you try does not exactly work out for you. However, it merits investing energy choosing which one to sign up within the beginning.

Utilizing the right agent truly can positively affect your trading. Online dealers are continually improving and they generally make the entire procedure for purchasing and selling options substantially more effective and simple to do. That is just obvious, however, if you utilize one of the top brokers that are truly good at giving a five-star service.

The procedure for picking a broker is not hard, however, there is a ton to consider. There are such huge numbers of decisions out there and although they all offer a similar sort of service, some of them may be more reasonable for you than others. Not every trader is going to have exactly the very same prerequisites which makes it extremely hard to say that a particular dealer is "the best." What may be directly for one broker may not be right for another.

The key is truly to work out what is essential to you and afterward do some examination to discover which specialist is probably going to be the most useful for your very own needs. We have a segment devoted to the Best Options Brokers that you may like to investigate, however, we would propose that you originally read through this page where we have covered a portion of the primary factors that you ought to consider.

- Quality and Speed of Order Execution
- Commissions and Fees
- Security Measures
- Trading Platform and Ease of Use
- Reputation
- Additional Considerations
- Customer Support

Commissions and Fees

It's to some level logical that one of the most significant contemplations while picking an online dealer or broker is what that the charges are. Charges can essentially be separated into two primary classifications: commissions and other fees.

Commissions are charged on each exchange that you make, whether you are purchasing or selling options, thus it can mean a sizable sum if you are making a lot of transactions. A few brokers likewise have a base commission and this is something to pay special mind to if you are planning to make various little exchanges; some may charge higher commissions relying upon what sort of option is being transacted.

The extra fees can envelop an entire scope of various charges including a yearly charge just for having an account, charges for withdrawals and deposits, or additional expenses for making particular sorts of orders.

Contingent upon what strategies and trading styles you are utilizing, you might be making exchanges that will just generate profits that are moderately little contrasted with the sum contributed. It isn't at all remarkable for options traders to work on very tight edges, and this makes it critical to decrease the costs associated with making trades.

Even if you will, in general, make trades that have higher margins, there is as yet a conspicuous advantage to decreasing costs because, quite basically, lower costs mean more profit. Perhaps the greatest cost engaged with trading options is, similarly as with any budgetary instrument, obviously the fees and commissions that are incurred when making a trade.

Hence, before you sign up at a broker you ought to know about their commission structure and any extra expenses that can be applied so you can be certain that their charges are reasonable for how you will be trading. However, it's likewise important that commissions and charges are not the ends of it. They are significant, however somewhat the facts confirm that you get what you pay for. The least expensive brokers are not the best, and it tends to merit paying somewhat more if you feel a more costly broker is better for you in other zones.

One specific reason behind paying more would be if you needed some assistance while you were beginning. Most online dealers are known as discount agents since they keep their commissions low and their service is essentially just to transact the orders that you tell them to. There are also full-service merchants, which regularly charge at a higher rate, yet give you the advantage of an experienced proficient on hand to offer you guidance and advice.

Such help can wind up being priceless, so a full-service broker may be worth considering; you can generally change to a discount agent once you gain the confidence and experience to do it alone.

Quality and Speed of Order Execution

The speed of which an online broker can implement your orders is another key factor that ought to be considered. If your broker does not carry out your transactions in an appropriate fashion, it can negatively affect how your order is filled and may even bring about your order not getting filled by any stretch of the imagination. The best ones will normally execute your orders as fast as could reasonably be expected and will be able to guarantee you that they are transacted at the most ideal price. Getting the most perfect prices available can have a major effect on your bottom line, so this truly is something you want to be done well.

On a comparable note, you also might need to utilize an online broker that has a quick and responsive site as the options market can move rapidly in fact. If your broker's site is refreshing too slowly, or you are encountering a delay when attempting to move between one page and another, this can lead to diminished profits, significant losses, or even missed opportunities if you are trying to place an order.

Although not explicitly identified with picking a broker, this is a suitable time to refer to the significance of having modern technology. You ought to have decent modern hardware and a solid internet if you will be trading options on the web.

Trading Platform & Ease of Use

Options trading is complex enough without the additional inconveniences of utilizing an online dealer that has a trading platform that is difficult to utilize. The last thing you need to do is have to invest any additional energy making sense of how to discover the information you are searching for or going through an exhausting procedure for placing in your orders. You truly want to utilize a broker that has an easy to use interface, a simple ordering method, and different highlights that help with overall functionality.

Security Measures

If you have an account with an online agent and you have your own money held up with them, you need to be certain that your account is secure and not at risk to be hacked. Sadly, that is a current risk that comes with utilizing online technology to make financial transactions. The top online merchants utilize the most recent safety measures to guarantee that they are totally protected from external interference and that your account and any private details that you give stay safe constantly.

Reputation

The best online brokers will, for the most part, have gained reputations for themselves and have solid track records of offering great support to their customers. If you stick to utilizing those that have great reputations, then the odds are high that you will have a positive experience.

Before you open an account with anybody, you should seriously think about doing a web search and checking whether there is negative feedback about them anywhere on the web. On the other hand, you should ensure that you just sign up with an organization that comes suggested by a reputable source, for example, the online brokers that are in this book.

Customer Support

Although you would trust that everything goes easily at all times, the odds are that you will experience some specialized challenges or issues or the like at some point. This is the reason the level of customer support offered by an agent or broker is likewise a factor worth considering. If you are using a decent one, at that point any issues will most likely be rare, but they will, in any case, happen sporadically and it's ideal to realize that there is decent customer service available to give you some help when you need it.

Additional Considerations

The previously mentioned factors are presumably the most significant, however, some extra contemplations are also worth considering. For instance, your trading plan may be based totally on trading options however there might be an odd event when you need to enhance and invest in other financial instruments. If you think this is probable, at that point you should be taking a look at brokers that are also reasonable for purchasing and selling other financial instruments.

You may likewise want to consider what choices are accessible if you can't make your trades online. If you have to make a trade, but don't approach the web, at that point you would need an alternative method for setting orders. If this is something that you think could be an issue for you then you ought to consider brokers that offer different approaches to make trades and communicate.

There are additionally several monetary related contemplations. Something that may be especially important for beginner traders is the base amount of deposit needed. Various online agents have high minimum deposit sums, and if you are planning on beginning with a moderately low starting capital, then this could be an issue for you. You should look at what the minimum deposit is before signing up anywhere, and guarantee that it's an appropriate sum for your budget.

The other financial related concern is what incentives may accessible. Since there are such a large number of online merchants around, the market place has become competitive and brokers are continually trying new advantages to pull in more clients. One way they do this is by offering traders incentives for signing with them.

Such incentives can incorporate decreased or free commissions for a while or some free funds added to your first deposit. A little bit of free money is not sufficient explanation without anyone else to pick a specific broker except if they also meet the most of your different prerequisites, but if you are struggling to pick between two agents/brokers, then going with the one with the best sign up offer is certainly not an awful method to choose. Be aware, however, that these incentives usually come with certain terms and conditions so you should ensure you realize what commitments you need to make.

The last factor that you may need to consider is the trading levels that are available to you. Whether this is pertinent to you to a great extent relies upon precisely how you plan on utilizing options contracts. If you just plan on utilizing options as part of a hedging strategy, to secure a current portfolio, at that point trading levels won't generally apply to you.

Every online broker will permit you to buy put options or write call options on basic securities that you effectively own because, you aren't generally facing any extra challenge, however just hedging against your securities falling in value. In any case, if you plan on utilizing options theoretically without possessing the pertinent underlying security, then trading levels will be a problem for you.

If you only plan on purchasing options with the end goal of practicing or selling them for a profit, then most brokers will likewise permit you to do that, giving you have the funds to do as such. If you are utilizing methodologies that involve writing options and therefore options margin, at that point trading levels are something you have to consider.

At the point when you sign up with an options broker, they will complete a risk appraisal to figure out what level of risk is reasonable for you, and your account will then be relegated a specific trading level. This will specify the suitable level of options margin and somewhat will impact what methodologies you can utilize. In this way, if you are planning on utilizing some of the more intricate procedures that require options margin, you need to take a look at what the prerequisites are of an online broker for being appointed to the trading level that you need.

Chapter 3:
RISK AND MONEY MANAGEMENT

Effectively dealing with your capital and risk exposure is basic when trading options. While risk is unavoidable with any type of investment, your exposure to risk doesn't need to be an issue. The key is to deal with the risk funds viably; constantly ensure that you are alright with the level of risk being taken and that you are not exposing yourself to unreasonable losses.

Similar ideas can be applied while dealing with your money as well. You ought to be trading utilizing capital that you can afford to lose; abstain from overstretching yourself. As effective money and risk management are completely vital to fruitful options trading, it's a subject that you truly need to comprehend. We will take a look at a portion of the techniques you can, and should, use for controlling your budget and managing your risk exposure.

- Managing Risk with Options Spreads
- Managing Risk Using Options Orders
- Managing Risk through Diversification
- Using Your Trading Plan
- Money Management & Position Sizing

Using Your Trading Plan

It's imperative to have a nitty-gritty trading plan that spreads out rules and parameters for your trading exercises. One of the pragmatic uses of such a plan is to assist you in dealing with your money and your risk exposure. Your plan ought to incorporate details of what level of risk you are OK with and the amount of capital you need to utilize.

By following your plan and just utilizing the money that you have explicitly distributed for options trading, you can keep away from probably the greatest mix-up that traders and investors make: utilizing "scared" money.

When you are trading with money that you either can not afford to lose or ought to have saved for other purposes, you are far less inclined to settle on rational choices in your exchanges. While it's hard to remove the emotion involved with options trading, you truly want to be as centered as conceivable around what you are doing and why.

When emotion assumes control over, you possibly begin to lose your concentration and are obligated to behave irrationally. It might make you pursue losses from past trades turned sour, for instance, or making transactions that you wouldn't generally make. If you follow your plan and stick to utilizing your investment capital then you should have a greatly improved potential for the success of monitoring your emotions.

Similarly, you should stick to the levels of risk that you diagram in your plan. If you want to make low-risk trades, at that point there truly is no reason behind why you should begin exposing yourself to more elevated levels of risk. It's frequently enticing to do this, maybe because you have made a couple of losses and you need to attempt to fix them, or possibly you have done well with some low-risk trades and need to begin expanding your profits at a quicker rate.

However, if you intended to make low-risk trades, then you did as such for a reason, and there is no reason for taking yourself from your comfort zone due to the same emotional reasons referenced above.

Managing Risk with Options Spreads

Options spreads are substantial and essential apparatuses in options trading. An option spread is essentially when you join more than one position on options contracts dependent on the same fundamental security to viably create one overall trading position.

For instance, if you purchased in the money calls on a particular stock and then wrote less expensive out of the money calls on the same stock, at that point, you would have made a spread known as a bull call spread. Purchasing the calls implies you stand to pick up if the hidden stock goes up in value, however you would lose a few or the entirety of the money spent to get them if the cost of the stock failed to go up. By composing calls on the same stock you would have the option to control a portion of the underlying costs and in this way lessen the maximum amount of money you could lose.

All options trading methodologies involve the utilization of spreads, and these spreads represent a valuable method to manage risk. You can utilize them to diminish the upfront costs of entering a position and to limit how much money you stand to lose, similarly as with the bull call spread model given above. This implies you possibly diminish the benefits you would make, however it lessens the general risk.

Spreads can likewise be utilized to lessen the risks involved when entering a short position. For instance, if you wrote in the money puts on stock, at that point you would get an upfront payment for writing those options, however, you would be exposed to potential losses if the stock dropped in value. If you likewise purchased less expensive out of money puts, then you would need to invest a portion of your upfront payment, however, you would top any potential losses that a decrease in the stock would cause. This exact kind of spread is called a bull put spread.

As should be obvious from both these models, it's possible to enter positions where you despite everything stand to gain if the price moves the right way for you, but you can carefully restrain any losses you may incur if the price moves against you. This is the reason spreads are so broadly utilized by options traders; they are incredible devices for risk management.

There is an enormous scope of spreads that can be utilized to take advantage or pretty much any market situation.

Managing Risk Through Diversification

Diversification is a risk management strategy that is regularly utilized by financial specialists that are building a portfolio of stocks by utilizing a purchase and hold technique. The essential standard of diversification for such investors is that spreading investments over various organizations and segments makes a reasonable portfolio as opposed to having a lot of money tied up in one specific organization or sector. A diversified portfolio is commonly viewed as less exposed to risk than a portfolio that is made up to a great extent of one explicit sort of investment.

With regards to options, diversification isn't significant in an incredible same way; anyway, it does still have its uses and you can diversify in various manners. Although the fact that the to a great extent continues as before, you don't need a lot of your capital committed on one specific type of investment, diversification is utilized in options trading through an assortment of techniques.

You can diversify by utilizing a selection of various procedures, by trading options that depend on a scope of basic securities, and by trading various sorts of options. Utilizing expansion is that you remain to make profits in various ways and you are not altogether dependent on one specific result for every one of your trades to be successful.

Managing Risk Using Options Orders

A moderately basic way to manage risk is to use the scope of various orders that you can place. Also, the four fundamental order types that you use to open and close situations, there are some of the extra orders that you can place, and a considerable lot of these can help you with risk management.

For instance, a typical market order will be filled at the best accessible price at the hour of execution. This is a consummately typical approach to purchase and sell options, however, in a volatile market, your order may wind up getting filled at a value that is higher or lower than you need it to be. By utilizing limit orders, where you can set maximum and minimum prices at which your order can be filled, you can abstain from purchasing or selling at less ideal prices.

There are orders that you can utilize to motorize leaving a position: whether to lock a profit already made or cut losses on a trade that didn't turn out well.

By utilizing orders, for example, the cutoff stop order, the trailing stop order, or the market stop order, you can easily control what you leave a position.

This will assist you with avoiding situations where you miss out on profits by holding on to a position for a long time or incur large losses by not closing out on a terrible position rapidly enough. By utilizing options orders suitably, you can restrict the risk you are presented to on every single trade you make.

Money Management and Position Sizing

Managing your money is inseparably connected to managing risk and both are similarly significant. You, at last, have a limited amount of money to utilize, and because it's crucial to keep tight control of your capital budget and to ensure that you don't lose everything and get yourself incapable to make additional trades.

The absolute most ideal approach to deal with your money is to utilize a genuinely simple idea known as position sizing. Position sizing is essentially choosing the amount of your capital you want to use to enter a specific position.

To viably utilize position sizing, you have to think about how much to invest in every individual trade in terms of a percentage of your general investment capital. In numerous regards, position sizing is a type of diversification. By just utilizing a little percentage of your capital in any one trade, you will never be too dependent on one explicit result. Even the best traders will make trades that turn out badly; the key is to make sure the awful ones don't affect you severely.

For instance, if you have 50 percent of your investment capital tied up in one trade and it winds up losing you money, then you will have most likely lost a lot of your available funds. If you keep an eye on just utilizing 5% to 10% of your capital per trade, at that point even a couple of consecutive losing trades shouldn't clear you out.

If you are sure that your trading plan will be effective over the long haul, then you should have the option to traverse the bad periods and still have enough capital to make something happen. Position sizing will assist you in doing precisely that.

Chapter 4:
OPTIONS TRADING STRATEGIES

There are many options trading techniques that can be utilized in the present trading scene. One of the most mainstream options trading strategies depends on Butterflies and Spreads. We should see them in detail.

Spreads and Butterflies

Spread trading is simultaneously purchasing and selling a similar option class however with various strike price and expiration dates. Spread options trading is utilized to constrain the risk, but then again, it also restrains the reward for the individual who enjoys spread trading.

Subsequently, if we are just keen on purchasing and selling call options of security, we will consider it a call spread, and if it is just put, then it will be known as a put spread.

Contingent upon the evolving factor, spreads can be sorted as:

- Horizontal Spread – Same Strike Price, Different expirations date
- Vertical Spread – Different Strike price. Same Expiration date
- Diagonal Spread - Different Strike price, Different expiration date

Recollect that an option's worth depends on the underlying security (for this situation, stock price). In this manner, we can likewise recognize an option spread on whether we need the cost to go down (Bear spread) or go up (Bull spread).

Bull call spread

In a bull call spread, we purchase more than one option to balance the potential loss if the exchange doesn't go our direction.

You may have had achievement beating the market by trading stocks utilizing a restrained procedure foreseeing a pleasant move either up or down. Numerous traders have likewise picked up the confidence to bring in money in the stock market by distinguishing a couple of good stocks presented to make a major move soon. However, if you don't have the foggiest idea of how to take advantage of that movement, you may be left in the dust. If this seems like you, possibly it's a great opportunity to consider utilizing options.

OPTION PRICING MODELS

Before wandering into the world of trading options, financial specialists ought to have a good comprehension of the components deciding the value of an option. These incorporate the present stock value, the intrinsic value, the time value or the time of expiration, interest rate, cash dividends paid, and volatility.

There are a few options pricing models that utilize these parameters to decide the fair market value of an option. Of these, the Black-Scholes model is the most generally known. In numerous ways, options are much the same as some other investment—you have to comprehend what determines their cost to utilize them viably. Different models are likewise ordinarily utilized, for example, the trinomial model and the binomial model.

How about we start with the essential drivers of the cost of an option: ebb and flow stock cost, inherent worth, time to lapse or time worth, and instability. The present stock cost is genuinely direct. The movement of the cost of the stock down or up has a direct, although not equivalent, impact on the cost of the option. As the price of stock ascents, the more likely it is that the cost of a call option will rise and the cost of a put option will fall. If the stock cost goes down, the opposite will undoubtedly happen to the cost/price of the calls and puts.

The Black-Scholes Formula

The Black Scholes model is maybe the most popular option pricing strategy. The model's formula is inferred by multiplying the stock cost/price by the aggregate standard typical probability distribution function. From that point, the net present value (NPV) of the strike price multiplied by the aggregate standard normal distribution is deducted from the resulting value of the previous computation.

The math involved with several equation that makes up the Black-Scholes equation can be intimidating and complicated. Luckily, you don't have to know or even comprehend the math to utilize Black-Scholes modeling in your own techniques. Options traders and speculators have access to an assortment of online options calculators, and a significant number of the today's trading platforms boast powerful options analysis apparatuses, including spreadsheets and indicators that perform the figurings and yield the options pricing values. However, how about we dig a little more profound into options prices to comprehend what makes up its extrinsic vs. intrinsic - which is clearer.

Intrinsic Value

Intrinsic value is the value any given option would have if it were practiced today. Fundamentally, the intrinsic value is the sum by which the strike cost of an option is profitable or in-the-money when contrasted with the stock's cost in the market. If the strike cost of the option isn't beneficial when contrasted with the cost of the stock, the option is said to be out-of-the-money. If the strike cost is equivalent to the stock's cost in the market, the option is said to be at-the-money.

Although intrinsic value incorporates the connection between the strike cost and the stock's cost in the market, it doesn't account for how little or how much is remaining until the option's lapse called the expiry. The measure of the time remaining on an option impacts the value or the premium of an option. In other words, intrinsic value is the bit of an option's cost not lost or affected because of the passage of time.

The intrinsic value of an option mirrors the viable financial advantage resulting from the prompt exercise of that option. Essentially, it is an option's base worth. Options trading out of the money or at the money or, have no intrinsic value.

Example of Intrinsic Value

For instance, suppose General Electric (GE) stock is selling at $34.80. The GE 30 call option would have an intrinsic value of $4.80 ($34.80 − $30 = $4.80) in light of the fact that the option holder can practice the option to purchase GE shares at $30, at that point pivot and naturally sell them in the market for $34.80 for a profit of $4.80.

In a different model, the GE 35 call option would have an intrinsic value of zero ($34.80 − $35 = - $0.20) because the intrinsic value can't be negative. Intrinsic value additionally works a similar way for a put option. For instance, a GE 30 put option would have an intrinsic value of zero ($30 − $34.80 = -$4.80) because the intrinsic value can't be negative. Then again, a GE 35 put option would have an intrinsic value of $0.20 ($35 − $34.80 = $0.20).

Time Value

Since options contracts have a limited amount of time before they lapse, the amount of time remaining has money related worth associated with it–called time value. It is legitimately identified with how much time an option has until it lapses, just as the fluctuations or volatility in the stock's price.

The additional time an option has until it lapses, the greater the possibility it will wind up in the money. The time segment of an option decays exponentially. The real determination of the time value of an option is a genuinely complex equation. An option will lose 33% of its value during the first half of its life and 66% during the second half of its life. This is a significant concept for securities investors because the closer the option gets to termination, the more of a move in the basic security is required to affect the cost of the option.

The Calculation and Formula of Time Value

The formula below shows that time value is determined by deducting an option's premium from the intrinsic value of the option.

Time\ Value = Option\ Price-Intrinsic\ ValueTime Value=Option Price−Intrinsic Value

At the end of the day, the time esteem is what's left of the premium in the wake of computing the profitability between the strike cost and stock's cost in the market. Subsequently, the time value is regularly alluded to as an option's extrinsic value since time value is the sum by which the cost of an option surpasses the intrinsic value.

Time value is the risk premium the option seller requires to give the option purchaser the option to purchase or sell the stock up to the date the option lapses. It is like an insurance premium for the option; the higher the risk, the higher the expense to purchase the option.

Example of Time Value

Taking a look at the model from above, if GE is trading at $34.80 and the one-month-to-expiration GE 30 call option is trading at $5, the time value of the option is $0.20 ($5.00 - $4.80 = $0.20).

With GE trading at $34.80, a GE 30 call option trading at $6.85 with 9 months to termination has a time value of $2.05. ($6.85 - $4.80 = $2.05). Notice the intrinsic value is the equivalent; the distinction in the cost of a similar strike price option is the time value.

Volatility

An option's time value is additionally exceptionally subject to the volatility the market anticipates that the stock should show up to expire. Normally, stocks with high volatility have a higher likelihood for the option to be profitable or in-the-money by expiry. Subsequently, the time value as a part of the option's premium–is commonly higher to make up for the expanded possibility that the stock's cost could move past the strike cost and expire in-the-money. For stocks that are not expected to move a lot, the option's time value will be moderately low.

One of the measurements used to quantify volatile stocks is called beta. Beta estimates the volatility of stock when contrasted with the general market. Volatile stocks will, in general, have high betas principally because of the uncertainty of the cost of the stock before the option lapses. In any case, high beta stocks additionally carry more risk than low-beta stocks. In other words, volatility is a double-edged blade, which means it permits speculators the potential for critical returns, however, volatility can also prompt huge losses.

The impact of volatility is generally subjective and hard to evaluate. Luckily, there are a few calculations to help evaluate volatility. To make this more fascinating, a few sorts of volatility exist, with historical and implied being the most noted. At the point when investors take a look at volatility previously, it is called either statistical volatility or historical volatility.

Historical Volatility

Historical volatility (HV) assists you in determining the conceivable greatness of future moves of the basic stock. Measurably, 66% of all occurrences of a stock cost will occur within minus or plus one standard deviation of the stock's move over a given period. Historical volatility looks back to show how unstable the market has been. This helps options financial specialists to figure out which exercise cost is generally suitable to decide for a specific strategy.

Implied Volatility

Implied volatility is what is implied by the present market costs and is utilized with hypothetical models. It helps set the present cost of a current option and enables options players to survey the potential of an exchange. Implied volatility estimates what options traders expect future instability will be. All things considered, implied volatility is a pointer of the present assessment of the market. This notion will be reflected in the cost of the options, helping traders evaluate the future volatility of the option and the stock dependent on current option costs.

FACTORS THAT DETERMINE OPTION PRICING

Options can be utilized in a wide assortment of techniques, from moderate to high risk. They can likewise be custom-made to meet expectations that go past basic directional techniques. Along these lines, when you learn essential options terminology, it bodes well to explore factors that influence an option's cost in various situations.

Utilizing Options For Directional Strategies

At the point when stock traders initially start utilizing options, it is for the most part to buy a call or a put for directional trading, where they expect a stock will move a specific way. These traders may pick an option as opposed to the fundamental stock because of restricted risk, high reward potential, and less capital required to control a similar number of shares.

If the standpoint is positive, purchasing a call option makes the opportunity to share in the upside potential without gambling more than a small amount of the market value. If bearish, purchasing a put lets the trade exploit a fall without the margin required to undercut.

Market Value and Direction

Numerous sorts of options strategies can be developed but the position's failure or success relies upon an intensive comprehension of the two kinds of options: the call and the put. Besides, taking full advantage options requires another perspective since traders who think exclusively in terms of market direction pass up on a wide range of opportunities.

In addition to going up or down, stocks can move sideways or trend unobtrusively higher or lower for long periods. They can likewise make substantial goes up or down in value, at that point switch bearing and end up back where they began. These sorts of value movements cause migraines for stock traders but give options traders the exclusive opportunity to bring in money even if the stock goes nowhere. Straddles, butterflies, strangles, and calendar spreads highlight a couple of options strategies intended to profit in those sorts of circumstances.

Chapter 5:
BASICS OF OPTION PRICING

Options traders need to comprehend extra factors that influence an option's price and the complexity of picking the right technique. When a stockbroker turns out to be acceptable at foreseeing the future price movement. the person may believe it is a simple change from options, but this isn't accurate. Options traders must deal with 3 shifting parameters that influence the price: the price of the underlying time, volatility, and security. Changes in any of these factors influence the option's value.

Option pricing hypothesis utilizes factors (exercise price, stock price, interest rate, time to expiration, volatility) to hypothetically value an option. It gives an estimation of an option's reasonable value which traders join into their techniques to maximize profits. Some ordinarily utilized models to value options are Black-Scholes, Monte-Carlo, and Binomial Option Pricing. These speculations have wide margins for error because of deriving their values from different assets, typically the cost of an organization's basic stock. There are scientific formulas intended to compute the fair reasonable value of an option. The broker simply inputs known factors and finds a solution that depicts what the option should be worth.

The essential objective of any option pricing model is to compute the probability that an option will be worked out, or be in-the-money (ITM), at lapse. Basic asset value (stock value), interest rate, exercise price, time to expiration, and volatility, which is the number of days between the computation date and the option's exercise date, are usually utilized variables that are input into logical models to derive an option's hypothetical fair value.

KEY PRICING INPUTS

Here are the general impacts that factors have on an option's cost:

Strike Price and Underlying Price

The value of puts and cuts are influenced by changes in the fundamental stock cost in a generally clear manner. At the point when the stock cost goes up, calls should gain in value since you can purchase the underlying asset at a lower cost than where the market is, and puts should diminish. In like manner, put options should increase in value, and calls should drop as the stock value falls, as the put holder gives the right to sell stock at costs over the falling market cost.

That pre-determined price at which to purchase or sell is known as the option's exercise price or strike price. If the strike price permits you to purchase or sell the basic at a level which allows for a quick profits purchase discarding that exchange in the open market, the option is in-the-money (for instance a call to purchase shares at $10 when the market cost is currently $15, you can make a prompt $5 profit).

Time to Expiration

The impact of time is easy to conceptualize yet takes understanding before understanding its effect because of the expiration date. Time works in the stock broker's favor since acceptable organizations tend to the ascent over significant periods. However, time is the adversary of the purchaser of the option because, if days go without a huge change in the price of the underlying, the price of the option will decrease. Likewise, the value of an option will decrease all the more quickly as it moves toward the expiration date. Alternately, that is uplifting news for the option seller, who attempts to profit by time decay, particularly during the last month when it happens most quickly.

3. Interest Rates

Like most other monetary resources, options costs are affected by prevailing interest rates and are affected by interest rate changes. Put option and call option premiums are affected contrarily as interest rates change: lose value while calls benefit from rising rates. The inverse is genuine when interest rates fall.

4. Volatility

The impact of volatility on an option's price is the most difficult concept for beginners to comprehend. It depends on a measure called statistical (also known as historical) volatility, SV for short, taking a look at past value developments of the stock over a given timeframe.

Option pricing models necessitate the trader to enter future volatility during the life of the option. Normally, option traders don't generally know what it will be and need to guess by working the pricing model "in reverse". All things considered, the merchant knows the cost at which the option is trading and can inspect different factors including dividends, interest rates, and time left with a bit of research. Subsequently, the main missing number will be future volatility, which can be evaluated from different information sources.

These inputs structure the center of implied volatility, a key measure utilized by option traders. It is known as implied volatility (IV) since it permits traders to figure out what they think future volatility is probably going to be.

Traders use IV to check if options are cheap or costly. You may hear option traders state that premium levels are high or that top-notch levels are low. What they truly mean is that the present IV is high or low. When comprehended, the dealer can decide when it is a decent time to purchase options - because premiums are modest - and when it is a decent time to sell options – because they are costly.

Options are unpredictable, yet their price can be portrayed by only a bunch of factors, the vast majority of which are known ahead of time. Just the volatility of the basic resource remains a matter of estimation. When you have a firm grasp of the fundamentals, you'll see that options flexibility to tailor the reward and risk of each exchange to your techniques.

7 FACTORS THAT AFFECT AN OPTION'S PRICE

You can't know where you are going until you realize where you've been. You can not price an option until you realize what makes up its worth. An options trade can turn into a mind-boggling machine of legs, numerous orders, Greeks, and adjustments, however, if you don't have the foggiest idea about the essentials, then what are you attempting to achieve?

When you take a look at an option chain have you at any point considered how they generated every one of those prices for the options? These options are not created randomly, however rather calculated out utilizing a model, for example, the Black-Scholes Model. We will dive further into the 7 components of the Black-Scholes Model and how and why they are utilized to determine an option's cost/price. Like all models, the Black-Scholes Model has a shortcoming and is a long way from perfect.

History Of The Black-Scholes Model

The Black-Scholes Model was distributed in 1973 as The Pricing of Options and Corporate Liabilities in the Journal of Political Economy. It was created by Myron Scholes and Fisher Black as an approach to evaluate the price of an option after some time. Robert Merton later distributed a subsequent paper further extending the comprehension of the model. Merton is credited for naming the model "Dark Scholes." In 1997, Merton and Scholes got the Nobel Prize for their work with the model. Fisher Black was not qualified because the Nobel Prize can't be granted after death.

As with any model, some assumptions have to be understood.

- As with any model, a few assumptions must be comprehended.

The rate of profit for the riskless asset is constant

- The underlying follows the more the option will be worth which expresses that move in an unpredictable and random path
- There is no riskless profit, arbitrage, opportunity
- It is possible to lend and borrow any amount of money at the riskless rate
- It is possible to purchase or short any amount of stock
- There are no charges or cost

There are seven factors in the model: strike price, stock price, interest rates, types of option, dividends, time of expiration, and future volatility. Of the seven elements, just one isn't known with any certainty: future volatility. This is the fundamental zone where the model can skew the outcomes.

1. Stock Price

If a call option permits you to purchase a stock at a predetermined cost later on than the higher that cost goes, the more the option will be worth.

Which option would have a higher worth:

- A call option permits you to purchase The Option Prophet (sym: TOP) for $100 while it is trading at $80 or
- A call option will enable you to buy TOP for $100 while it is trading at $120

Nobody is going to pay $100 for something they can purchase on the open market for $80, so our option in Choice 1 will have a low worth.

What is all the more alluring is Choice 2, an option to purchase TOP for $100 when its worth is $120. In this circumstance, our option worth will be higher.

2. Strike Price

Strike price follows the same lines from the stock price. At the point when we group strikes, we do it as in-the-money, at-the-money or out-of-the-money. When a call option is in-the-money, it implies the stock price/cost is higher than the strike cost. When a call is out-of-the-money, the stock price is not exactly the strike price.

A TOP call has a strike of fifty while TOP is presently trading at $60, this option is in-the-money.

On the other side of that coin, a put option is in-the-money when the stock price is not exactly the strike price. A put option is out-of-the-money when the stock price is greater than the strike price.

A TOP put has a strike of twenty while TOP is presently trading at $40, this option is out-of-the-money.

In-the-money options have a greater value contrasted with out-of-the-money options.

3. Type Of Option

This is likely the easiest factor to comprehend. An option is either a call or a put, and the estimation of the option will change appropriately.

- A call option gives the holder the option or right to purchase the basic at a predefined cost within a particular timeframe.
- A put option gives the holder the option or right to sell the hidden at a predefined price within a particular timeframe.

If you are long a call or short a put your option value increments as the market moves higher. If you are short a call or long a put your option value increments as the market goes lower.

4. Time To Expiration

Options have a constrained life expectancy, thus their worth is influenced by the progression of time. As the time to expiration upturns the value of the option increments. As the time to termination draws nearer the value of the option starts to diminish. The value starts to quickly diminish within the last 30 days of an option's life. The additional time an option has till termination/expiration, the additional time the option needs to move around.

5. Interest Rates

Interest rate has a nominal effect on an option's value. At the point when interest rates rise a call option's value will likewise rise, and a put option's value will decrease.

To drive this idea home, how about we take a look at the dynamic procedure of attempting to invest in TOP while it is trading at $50.

- We can purchase 100 shares of the stock altogether which would cost us $5,000.
- Instead of purchasing the stock altogether, we can get long an at-the-money call for $5.00. Our all-out expense here would be $500. Our underlying cost of money would be littler, and this would leave us $4,500 leftover. Also, we will have a similar prize potential for half the risk. Presently we can take that additional money and invest it somewhere else, for example, Treasury Bills. This would create a guaranteed return on our investment in TOP.

The higher the interest rate, the more appealing the subsequent option becomes. In this manner, when interest rates go up, calls are a superior investment, so their cost likewise increments.

On the other side of that coin, if we take a look at a long put versus a long call, we can see an impediment. We have 2 options when we want to play an underlying drawback.

- You can short a hundred shares of the stock which would produce money into the business and let us earn interest on that money.

- You long a put which will cost you less money by and large but not put additional money into your business that produces interest income.

The higher the interest rate, the more appealing the primary option becomes. Accordingly, when interest rates rise, the value of put options decreases.

6. Dividends

Options don't get dividends, so their value varies when profits are discharged. When an organization discharges dividends, they have an ex-dividend date. If you own the stock on that date, you will be granted the dividend. Additionally on this date, the estimation of the stock will diminish by the number of dividends. As dividends increment a put option's value likewise increments and a calls' value declines.

7. Volatility

Volatility is the main evaluated factor in this model. The volatility that is utilized is forward volatility. Forward volatility is the proportion of implied volatility over a period later on.

Implied volatility shows the "simplified" development in a stock's future volatility. It discloses to you how traders think the stock will move. Implied volatility is constantly communicated as a percentage, non-directional, and on a yearly premise.

The higher the implied volatility, the more individuals figure the stock's price will move. Stocks recorded on the Dow Jones are value stocks, so a ton of development isn't normal. In this manner, they have lower implied volatility. Growth stocks or little tops found on the Russell 2000, on the other hand, are required to move around a ton, so they convey higher implied volatility.

The Black-Scholes Model is utilized to determine an option's value. While there are numerous presumptions in the equation, the Black-Scholes Model is as yet the most broadly utilized. Its simplicity of calculation and helpful approximation makes a solid premise to fabricate increasingly complex models. Out of the seven factors volatility is the one in particular that is evaluated. Out of the seven factors, the most significant are strike price, stock price, time of expiration, volatility, and type of option. Dividends and Interest rates have an extremely minute impact on an option's value.

Chapter 6:
THE GREEKS

What Are the Greeks?

G reeks" is a term utilized in the options market to portray the various dimensions of risk associated with taking an options position. These factors are called Greeks since they are regularly connected with Greek symbols. Each risk variable is a consequence of a flawed presumption or relationship of the option with another underlying variable. Traders utilize diverse Greek qualities, for example, theta, delta, and others, to evaluate options risk and oversee option portfolios.

KEY TAKEAWAYS

- The 'Greeks' allude to the different components of risk that an options position entails.
- Greeks are utilized by options portfolio and traders managers to hedge the risk and comprehend how their profit and loss will carry on as prices move.
- The most regular Greeks incorporate the Gamma, Delta, Vega, and Theta - which are the first partial subsidiaries of the options pricing model.

THE BASICS OF THE GREEKS

Greeks entail numerous factors. These incorporate delta, gamma, theta, rho, and vega, among others. Every last one of these factors/Greeks has a number related to it, and that number enlightens traders concerning how the option moves or the risk related to that option. The essential Greeks (Delta, Gamma, Vega, Rho, and Theta) are determined each as a first partial subsidiary of the options pricing model (for example, the Black-Scholes model).

The value or number related to Greek changes after some time. In this manner, modern options traders may ascertain these qualities every day to survey any progressions which may influence their outlook or position or to check if their portfolio should be rebalanced. The following are a few of the primary Greeks traders take a look at.

Delta

Delta (Δ) means the rate of change between the option's cost and a \$1 change in the underlying asset's price. As it were, the price sensitivity of the option comparative with the underlying. Delta of a call option has a range somewhere in the range of zero and one, while the delta of a put option has a range between zero and a negative one. For instance, assume an investor is long a call option with a delta of 0.50. In this manner, if the underlying stock increments by \$1, the option's cost would hypothetically increment by 50 cents.

For options traders, delta likewise represents the hedge ratio for making a delta-unbiased position. For instance, if you buy a standard American call option with a 0.40 delta, you should sell 40 shares of stock to be completely hedged. Net delta for options can likewise be utilized to get the portfolio's hedge ration.

Less basic utilization of an option's delta is it's the present probability that it will terminate in-the-money. For example, a 0.40 delta call option today has an implied 40% probability of completing in-the-money.

Theta

Theta (Θ) means the rate of change between the time and option price - in some cases known as an option's time decay. Theta shows the sum an option's price would diminish as the time to expiration diminishes, all else equivalent. For instance, assume an investor is long an option with a theta of - 0.50. The option's price would diminish by 50 cents daily, all else being equal.

Theta increments when options are at-the-money, and diminishes when options are in-and out-of-the-money. Options closer to lapse likewise have quickening time decay. Long puts and long calls will normally have negative Theta; short puts and calls will have positive Theta. By contrast, an instrument whose worth isn't dissolved by time, for example, a stock, would have zero Theta.

Gamma

Gamma (Γ) means the rate of change between an option's delta and the underlying asset's cost. This is called second-derivative price sensitivity. Gamma shows the sum the delta would change given a $1 move in the fundamental security. For instance, assume a financial specialist is a long one call option on speculative stock XYZ. The call option has a delta of 0.50 and a gamma of 0.10. In this manner, if stock XYZ increments or diminishes by \$1, the call option's delta would increment or decrease by 0.10.

Gamma is utilized to determine how steady an option's delta is: higher gamma values show that delta could change drastically in light of even little movements in the underlying's price. Gamma is higher for options that are at-the-money and lower for options that are in-and out-of-the-money and quickens in size as expiration draws near. Gamma values are commonly littler the further away from the date of expiration; options with extended expirations are less sensitive to delta changes. As expiration draws near, gamma values are ordinarily bigger, as price changes have more effect on gamma.

Options traders may select to hedge delta as well as gamma to be delta-gamma neutral, implying that as the underlying price moves, the delta will stay near zero.

Vega

Vega (v) implies the rate of change between the underlying asset's implied volatility and an option's value. This is the option's sensitivity to volatility. Vega demonstrates the sum of an option's value changes given a 1% change in implied volatility. For instance, an option with a Vega of 0.10 shows the option's worth is relied upon to change by 10 cents if the implied volatility changes by 1 percent.

Because expanded volatility infers that the underlying instrument is bound to encounter extreme values, an ascent in volatility will correspondingly build the value of an option. Alternately, a reduction in volatility will adversely influence the value of the option. Vega is at its most extreme for at-the-money options that have longer times until expiration.

Greek-language nerds will call attention to that there is no genuine Greek letter named vega. There are different hypotheses about how this symbol, which takes after the Greek letter nu, found its way into the stock-trading language.

Rho

Rho (p) implies the rate of change between an option's price and a 1% change in the interest rate. This estimates sensitivity to the interest rate. For instance, expect a call option has a rho of 0.05 and a cost of $1.25. If interest rate ascends by 1%, the estimation of the call option would increment to $1.30, all else being equal. The inverse is valid for put options. Rho is most prominent for at-the-money options with long times until termination/expiration.

Minor Greeks

Some different Greeks, which are not discussed often are epsilon, vomma, lambda, speed, vera, ultima, color, and zomma.

These Greeks are second-or third-subordinates of the pricing model and influence things, for example, the change in delta with a change in volatility, etc. They are progressively utilized in options trading strategies as computer programming can rapidly process and record for these complex and sometimes obscure risk factors.

Chapter 7:
STRANGLES AND STRADDLES

S trangles and Straddles are the two options techniques that permit an investor to profit by critical moves in a stock's price, whether the stock goes up or down. The two methodologies comprise of purchasing an equal number of put and call options with the same termination date. The difference is that the strangle has two diverse strike prices, while the straddle has a typical strike price.

Options are a type of subsidiary security, which means the cost of the options is intrinsically connected to the cost of something different. If you purchase an options contract, you have the right, however not the responsibility to purchase or sell an underlying asset at a set cost before a particular date.

A call option gives an investor the option to purchase stock, and a put option gives an investor the option to sell a stock. The strike price of an option contract is the cost at which an underlying stock can be purchased or sold. The stock must transcend this price for calls or fall underneath for puts before a position can be practiced for a profit.

KEY TAKEAWAYS

- Strangles and Straddles are options techniques investors use to profit by huge moves in a stock's value, paying little regard to the direction.

- Straddles are helpful when it's unclear what direction the stock price may move in, with the goal that way the investor is secured, paying little regard to the result.
- Strangles are valuable when the financial specialist believes it's likely that the stock will move one way or the other however needs to be protected in the event of some unforeseen circumstance.
- Investors ought to become familiar with the perplexing tax laws around how to account for options trading profit and losses.

Straddle

The straddle trade is one path for a broker to benefit from the price movement of an underlying asset. Suppose an organization is scheduled to discharge its most recent income results about three weeks, however, you have no clue whether the news will be positive or negative. These weeks before the news discharge would be a decent time to go into a straddle since when the outcomes are discharged, the stock is probably going to move sharply lower or higher.

How about we assume that the stock is trading at $15 in the period of April. Assume a $15 call option for June has a cost of $2, while the cost of the $15 put option for June is $1. A straddle is accomplished by purchasing both the put and the call for an aggregate of $300: ($2 + $1) x 100 shares for each option contract = $300.

The straddle will increment in price if the stock moves higher (due to the long call option) or if the stock goes lower (due to the long put option). Profits will be gotten as long as the price of the stock moves by more than $3 per share in either course.

Strangle

Another way to manage options is the strangle position. While a straddle has no directional inclination, a strangle is utilized when the financial specialist accepts the stock has a superior possibility of moving a specific direction, however, it might still like to be secured on account of a negative move.

For instance, suppose you believe an organization's outcomes will be positive, which means you require less downside protection. Rather than purchasing the put option with the strike price of $15 for $1, possibly you take a look at purchasing the $12.50 strike that has a cost of $0.25. This trade would cost less than the straddle and require less of an upward move for you to equal the initial investment (or break-even).

Utilizing the lower-strike put option in this strangle will still secure you against the outrageous downside, while likewise placing you in a superior position to pick up from a positive declaration.

These techniques consolidate put and call options to make positions where a speculator can benefit from price swings in the underlying stock, even when the financial specialist doesn't know what direction the price will swing.

In the straddle technique, a financial specialist or an investor holds a position in a put or call option with the same strike price and lapse dates for the same underlying stock. In the strangle technique, a speculator/investor holds a put and call option with the same termination dates however unique strike prices for the same underlying stock.

In a straddle position, an investor holds a put and call option that is "at-the-money." In a strangle position, a speculator/investor holds a put and call option that is "out-of-the-money." Due to this, getting into a strangle position is commonly less expensive than getting into a straddle position.

In the wake of taking a look at these two models, investors should understand how the straddle and strangle options work. These techniques are effective tools that can be utilized when an investor wants to profit from an unpredictable or volatile stock.

Chapter 8:
IRON CONDOR AND BUTTERFLY

What Is an Iron Condor?

An iron condor is an options technique made with four options comprising of two puts (one short and one long) and two calls (one short and one long), and four strike prices, all with the same termination date. The objective is to profit from low unpredictability in the underlying asset. At the end of the day, the iron condor procures the most extreme profit when the underlying asset closes between the center strike prices at expiration.

The iron condor has a comparative result as a normal condor spread, however, it utilizes both puts and calls rather than just calls or just puts. Both the condor and the iron condor are expansions of the iron butterfly and butterfly spread, respectively.

KEY TAKEAWAYS

- An iron condor is ordinarily an unbiased technique and profits the most when the underlying asset does not move a lot. Although, the technique can be developed with a bearish or bullish bias.
- The iron condor is made out of four options: a purchased put further OTM and a sold put nearer to the money, and a purchased call further OTM and a sold call nearer to the money.

- Profit is topped at the premium gotten while the risk is likewise topped at the contrast between the purchased and sold call strikes and the purchased and sold put strikes (less the premium got).

Understanding the Iron Condor

The technique has constrained upside and downside risk due to the low and high strike options, the wings, secure against noteworthy moves in either direction. Due to this constrained risk, its profit potential is likewise restricted. The commission can be an eminent factor here, as there are four options involved.

For this technique, the dealer in a perfect world might like all of the options to worthlessly expire, which is just conceivable if the underlying asset closes between the middle two-strike costs at termination. There will probably be an expense to close the trade if it is successful. If it isn't, the loss is still constrained.

One approach to think about an iron condor is having a long strangle within a bigger, short strangle (or the other way around).

The development of the strategy is as follows:

1. Buy one out of the money (OTM) put with a strike cost beneath the present cost of the underlying asset. The out of the money put option will secure against a huge downside move to the underlying asset.
2. Sell one OTM or at the money (ATM) put with a strike value nearer to the present cost of the underlying asset.
3. Sell one OTM or ATM call with a strike cost over the present cost of the underlying asset.

4. Buy one OTM call with a strike cost further over the present cost of the underlying asset. The out of the money call option will secure against a considerable upside move.

The options that are additionally out of money, known as the wings, are both long positions. Since both of these options are farther from the money, their premiums are lower than the two composed options, so there is a net credit to the record while placing the trade.

By choosing distinctive strike prices, it is conceivable to make the technique lean bearish or bullish. For instance, if both the center strike prices are over the present cost of the underlying asset, the dealer seeks after a little ascent in its cost by expiration. It still has limited risk and limited reward.

Iron Condor Losses and Profits

The most extreme profits for an iron condor is the amount of credit, or premium, gotten for making the four-leg options position.

The most extreme loss is likewise topped. The greatest loss is the contrast between the short call and long call strikes, or the short put and long put strikes. Lessen the shortfall by the net credits gotten, however, then add commissions to get the absolute loss for the trade.

The greatest loss occurs if the value moves over the long call strike (which is higher than the sold call strike) or underneath the long put strike (which is lower than the sold put strike).

Case of an Iron Condor on a Stock

Let's assume that an investor believes that Apple Inc. will be generally level in terms of price over the following two months.

They choose to actualize an iron condor. The stock is presently trading at $212.26.

They sell a call with a $215 strike, which gives them $7.63 in premium. They purchase a call with a strike of $220, which costs them $5.35. The credit on these 2 legs is $2.28, or $228 for one contract. The trade is just half complete, however.

Also, the broker sells a put with a strike of $210, which results in a premium gotten of $7.20. They additionally purchase a put with a strike of $205, costing $5.52. The net credit on these 2 legs is $1.68 or $168 if trading one contract on each.

The entire credit for the position is $3.96 ($2.28 + $1.68), or $396. This is the greatest profit the broker can make. This greatest profit occurs if all the options terminate worthless, which implies the cost must be somewhere in the range of $215 and $210 when termination occurs in two months. If the price is above $215 or beneath $210, the dealer could still make a diminished profit, however, it could likewise lose money.

The loss gets bigger if the price of Apple stock methodologies the upper call strike ($220) or the lower put strike ($205). The most extreme loss occurs if the cost of the stock trades above $220 or beneath $205.

Assume the stock at termination is $225. This is over the upper call strike value, which implies the broker is facing the most extreme conceivable loss. The sold call is losing $10 ($225 - $215) while the purchased call is making $5 ($225 - $220). The puts expire. The broker/trade loses $5, or $500 total, but they additionally got $396 in premiums. In this manner, the loss is topped at $104 in addition to commissions.

Let's assume the cost of Apple rather dropped, but not beneath the lower put threshold. It decreases to $208. The short call is losing $2 ($208 - $210), or $200, while the long put lapses useless. The calls additionally expire. The dealer loses $200 on the position, however, he got $396 in premium credits. In this way, they still make $196, fewer commission costs.

IRON BUTTERFLY

What is an Iron Butterfly?

An iron butterfly is an options trade that utilizes four distinct contracts as a feature of a technique to benefit from futures price or stocks that move within a characterized range. The trade is likewise developed to profit by a decrease in implied volatility. The way to utilizing this trade as a feature of an effective trading technique is conjecture when option costs are probably going to decrease in value generally. This normally happens during periods of a mild upward trend or sideways movement. The trade is also called "Iron Fly."

KEY TAKEAWAYS

- Iron Butterfly trades are utilized as an approach to benefit from price movement in a thin range during a time of reducing implied volatility.
- The development of the trade is like that of a short-straddle trade with a long put and long call option bought for protection.
- Traders should be aware of commissions to be certain they can utilize this strategy successfully in their accounts.
- Traders should know that his trade could prompt a broker to procure the stock after expiration.

How an Iron Butterfly Works

The Iron Butterfly trade is made with four options comprising of two put options and two call options. These puts and calls are spread out more than three strike prices, all with the same termination date. The objective is to profit from conditions where the value remains genuinely steady and the options exhibit declining historical and implied volatility.

It can likewise be thought of as a consolidated option trade utilizing both a long strangle and a short straddle, with the strangle positioned on two additional strikes below and above the middle strike price and the straddle positioned on the middle of the three-strikes price.

The trade receives the maximum profit when the underlying assets close precisely on the center strike price at the end of termination. A broker will build an Iron Butterfly trade with the following advances.

1. The broker initially distinguishes a price at which they forecast the underlying asset will lay on a given day later. This is the objective price.
2. The broker will utilize options that expire that day or close to that day they forecast the objective cost.
3. The broker gets one call option with a strike value well over the objective price. This call option is required to be out-of-the-money at the hour of expiration. It will secure against a critical upward move in the underlying asset and top any potential loss at a defined sum should the exchange/trade not go as forecast.
4. The broker sells both a put and a call option utilizing the strike cost nearest the objective cost or objective price. This strike price will be lower than the call option bought in the past step and higher than the put option in the subsequent step.

5. The broker gets one put option with a strike value well beneath the objective cost. This put option is required to be out-of-the-money at the hour of termination. It will protect against a significant descending move in the underlying asset and top any potential loss at a characterized sum should the trade not go as forecast.

The strike prices for the option contracts sold in steps three and two ought to be far enough apart to account for a scope of development in the underlying. This will permit the dealer to have the option to forecast the scope of effective value development instead of a thin range close to the objective price.

For instance, if the dealer feels that, throughout the following fourteen days, the underlying could land at the cost of $50, and be within a range of $5 higher or $5 lower from that target value, then the trader should sell a put and a call option with a strike price of $50 and should buy a call option at least $5 higher, and a put option at least $5 lower, than the $50 target cost. In principle, this makes a higher probability that the value action can land and stay in a beneficial range on or close to the day that the options expire.

Deconstructing the Iron Butterfly

The strategy has restricted the upside profit potential by structure. It is a credit-spread technique, implying that the dealer sells option premiums and takes credit for the price of the options at the beginning of the trade. The broker expects that the value of the options will lessen and culminate in an essentially lesser value, or no value at all. The broker in this manner plans to keep as much of the credit as could reasonably be expected.

The technique has characterized risk because of the low and high strike (the wings), protect against huge moves in either direction. It ought to be noticed that commission costs are constantly a factor with this technique since four options are involved. Traders will need to verify that the maximum potential profit isn't altogether dissolved by the commissions charged by their broker.

The Iron butterfly trade profits as lapse day draw near if the value lands within a range close to the middle strike price. The middle strike is where the merchant sells both a put option (a short strangle). The trade lessens in value as the price floats away from the middle strike, either lower or higher, and arrives at a point of maximum loss as the value moves either underneath the lower strike price or over the higher strike price.

Chapter 9:
HOW TO USE POPULAR OPTIONS STRATEGIES

Traders frequently bounce into trading options with little comprehension of options strategies. There are numerous strategies available that maximize return and limit risk. With a little exertion, traders can figure out how to take advantage of the power and flexibility options offered. Because of this, we've assembled this preliminary, which ought to shorten the learning curve and point you in the right way.

1. Covered Call

With calls, one technique is basically to purchase a naked call option. You can likewise structure a fundamental covered call or buy-write. This is a famous methodology since it generates income and decreases some danger of being long stock alone. The trade-off is that you should be eager to sell your shares at a set price: the short strike price. To execute the technique, you buy the underlying stock as you typically would, and simultaneously sell a call option on those same shares.

In this illustration, we are using a call option on a stock, which signifies a hundred portions of stock for each call option. For every hundred shares of stock you buy, you also sell 1 call option against it. It is implied as a covered call supposing that stock rockets are greater in esteem, your short call is secured by the long stock position.

Financial specialists may utilize this technique when they have a transient position in the stock and impartial opinion on its course. They may be hoping to generate income or protect against a potential decrease in the underlying stock's worth.

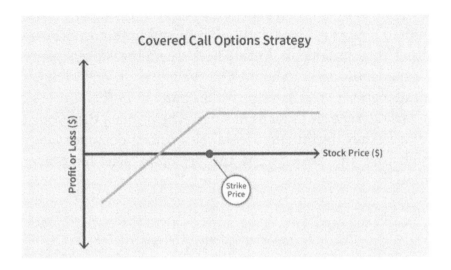

In the Profit and loss diagram above, notice how as the stock price rises, the negative Profit and loss from the call is counterbalanced by the position of the long share. Since you get premium from selling the call, as the stock travels through the strike price to the upside, the premium you got permits you to successfully sell your stock at a more elevated level than the strike price (premium received + strike). The covered call's Profit and loss chart look a great deal like a short naked put's Profit and loss chart.

2. Married Put

In a married put technique, an investor buys an asset (in this model, shares of stock), and simultaneously buy put options for an equal number of shares. The holder of a put option has the option to sell stock at the strike price. Each contract is worth a hundred shares. The reason a speculator or investor would utilize this strategy is basically to protect their downside risk when holding a stock. This approach functions just like an insurance technique, and sets up a value floor should the stock's value fall suddenly.

An instance of the married put would be if a dealer buys a hundred shares of stock and buys one put option at the same time. This technique is alluring because an investor is secured to the downside should a negative event happen. Simultaneously, the investor would partake in the entirety of the upside if the stock gains in value. The primary drawback to the procedure/technique occurs if the stock does not fall, in which case the dealer loses the premium paid for the put option.

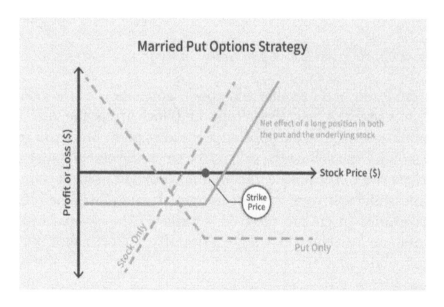

In the diagram above (profit and loss diagram), the dashed line is the long stock position.

With the long stock and long put positions joined, you can observe that as the stock price falls, the losses are constrained. However, the stock partakes in upside above the premium spent on the put. The married put's P and L graph is like a long long call's P and L diagram.

3. Bull Call Spread

In a bull call spread technique, a dealer will at the same time buy calls at a specific strike price and sell a comparable number of calls at a higher strike price.

Both call options will have the same underlying asset and expiration. This kind of vertical spread technique is frequently utilized when an investor is bullish on the underlying and anticipates a moderate ascent in the cost of the asset. The investor constrains his/her upside on the trade, yet lessens the net premium spent contrasted with purchasing a naked call option inside and out.

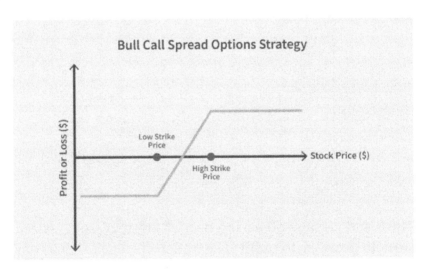

In the Profit and loss diagram above, you can see this is a bullish technique, so the broker needs the stock to increment in cost to make a profit on the trade.

The trade-off when placing a bull call spread is that your upside is limited, while your premium spent is lessened. If total calls are expensive, one way to deal with counterbalance the higher premium is by selling higher strike calls against them. This is the way a bull call spread is developed.

4. Bear Put Spread

The bear put spread strategy is another sort of vertical spread. In this technique, the investor will simultaneously purchase put options at a specific strike price and sell a comparative number of puts at a lesser strike price. The two options would be for a similar termination date and the same underlying asset. This strategy is utilized when the dealer/broker is bearish and foresees the fundamental asset's cost to drop. It offers both restricted gains and constrained losses.

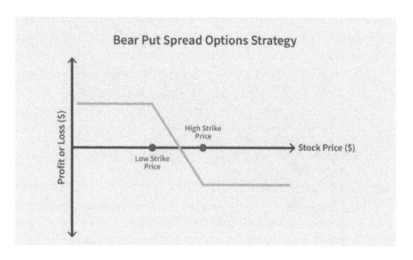

The P and L graph above is a bearish strategy, so you need the stock to decrease to profit. The trade-off while using a bear put spread is that your upside is confined, however, your premium spent is diminished. If absolute puts are and are expensive, one way to deal with counterbalance the high premium is by selling lower strike puts against them. This is how a bear put spread is developed.

5. Protective Collar

A protective collar technique is executed by purchasing an out-of-the-money put option and writing an out-of-the-money call option for the same basic asste and expiration.

This technique is frequently utilized by investors after a long position in a stock has experienced significant gains. This options mix permits investors to have downside assurance (long puts to secure profits) while having the trade-off of conceivably being committed to sell shares at a more significant price (selling higher = more profit than at current stock levels).

A basic model would be if an investor is long a hundred shares of IBM at $50 and IBM has ascended to $100 as of 1st of January.

The dealer could develop a protective collar by selling one IBM March 15th 105 calls and simultaneously buying one IBM March 95 put. The dealer is ensured below 95USD until the fifteenth of walk March, with the trade-off of perhaps committing to sell their shares at 105USD.

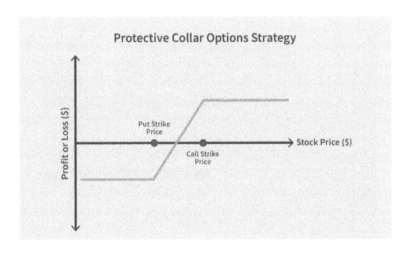

In the Profit and loss chart above, you can see that the protective collar is a blend of a long put and a covered call. This is an unprejudiced exchange set-up, inferring that you are ensured if there should arise an occurrence of falling stock, anyway with the trade-off of having the potential obligation to sell your long stock at the short call strike. however, the investor should be happy to do as such, as they have quite recently experienced gains in the basic shares.

6. Long Straddle

This strategy is the point at which an investor or a dealer simultaneously purchases a put and call option on the equivalent underlying asset, with a similar strike price and termination. An investor will often as possible use this method when the individual believes the cost of the fundamental/underlying asset will move out of a range, in any case, is unsure of which course the move will take. This methodology allows the investor to have the open door for speculatively limitless gain, while the most extreme loss is limited unmistakably to the expense of the two options contracts consolidated.

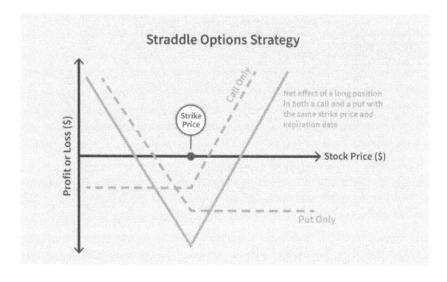

In the P and L diagram above, see how there are two breakeven points. This approach becomes beneficial when the stock makes an enormous move one direction or the other. The speculator or investor couldn't care less about which course the stock moves, only that it is a more noticeable move than the entire premium the investor paid for the structure.

7. Long Strangle

This is a strategy, the investor/speculator purchases an out-of-the-money call option and an out-of-the-money put option simultaneously on the same expiration, at the same time, and the same underlying asset.

An investor who utilizes this strategy accepts the underlying asset's price will encounter a huge movement however is uncertain of which direction the move will take.

This could, for instance, be a wager on an income discharge for an organization or an FDA event for a health care stock. Losses are restricted to the premium spent on the two options. Strangles will regularly be more affordable and reasonable than straddles because the options purchased are out of the money.

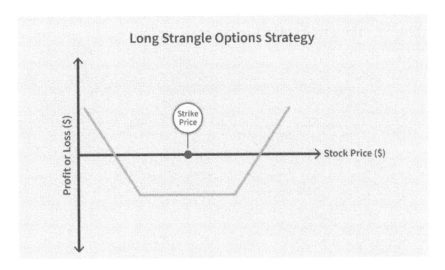

In the P and L diagram above, there are two breakeven points. This strategy becomes productive when the stock makes a particularly enormous move one way or the other. Again, the speculator couldn't think less about which course the stock moves, only that it is a more eminent move than the absolute premium the investor or speculator paid for the structure.

8. Long Call Butterfly Spread

The whole strategy so far has required a blend of two unique contracts or positions. In a long butterfly spread using call options, a speculator/investor will combine both a bull spread technique and a bear spread technique, and use three different strike price. All options are for the same underlying asset and termination date.

For example, a long butterfly spread can be developed by purchasing one in-the-money call option at a lower strike price, while purchasing one out-of-the-money call option, and selling two at-the-money call options. A reasonable butterfly spread will have a comparative wing widths. This model is called a "call fly" and results in a net debit. An investor/speculator would go into a long butterfly call spread when they figure the stock will not move much by expiration or termination.

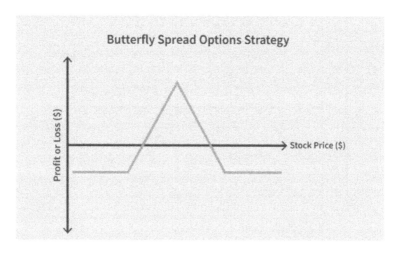

In the P and L diagram above, see how the most extreme gain is made when the stock remains unaltered up until termination

(straight at the ATM strike). The further away the stock moves from the ATM strikes, the more noticeable the negative change in P and L. Most extreme loss happens when the stock settles at or over the higher strike call, or when it settles at the lower strike or below, This strategy has both the constrained drawback and restricted upside.

9. Iron Condor

An intriguing technique is the iron condor. In this strategy, the investor/speculator simultaneously holds a bear call spread and a bull put spread. The iron condor is built by selling one out-of-the-money put and buying one out-of-the-money call of a higher strike (bear call spread), and selling one out-of-the-money put and buying one out-of-the-money put of a lower strike (bull put spread). All options have a comparative termination date and are on the same basic asset. Ordinarily, the call and put sides have a comparable spread width.

This trading technique earns a net premium on the structure and is intended to take advantage of a stock experiencing low unpredictability. Numerous traders like this trade for its apparent high likelihood of gaining a modest amount of premium.

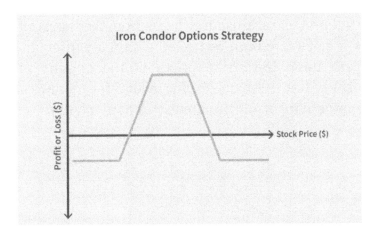

Iron Condor Options Strategy

In the Profit and loss chart above, see how the maximum gain is made when the stock stays unaltered up until termination (directly at the ATM strike). The further away the stock moves from the ATM strikes, the more noteworthy the negative change in Profit and loss. Maximum loss happens when the stock settles at the lower strike or underneath, or if the stock settles at or over the higher strike call. This procedure has both the limited downside and limited upside.

10.   Iron Butterfly

The last option strategy we will exhibit is the iron butterfly. In this technique, an investor will sell an at-the-money put and purchase an out-of-the-money put, while likewise selling an at-the-money get and purchasing an out-of-the-money call. All options have a similar expiration date and are on the equivalent underlying asset. Although like a butterfly spread, this strategy contrasts since it utilizes both puts and calls, rather than one or the other.

This strategy joins selling an at-the-money straddle and purchasing protective "wings." You can likewise think about the construction as two spreads. It isn't unexpected to have a similar width for the two spreads. The long out-of-the-money call protects against boundless drawbacks. The long out-of-the-money put protects against drawbacks from the short put strike to zero. P and L are both restricted within a particular range, contingent upon the strike prices of the options utilized. Investors like this technique for the income it generates and the higher probability of a little gain with a non-volatile stock.

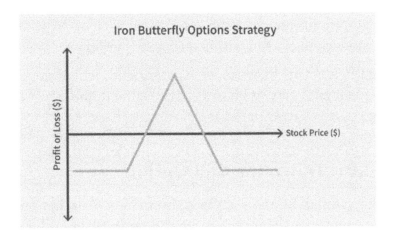

In the Profit and loss chart above, notice how the maximum gain is made when the stock stays unaltered up until expiration (directly at the ATM strike). The further the stock moves away from the ATM strikes, the more eminent the negative change in P and L. Greatest loss occurs when the stock settles at the lower strike, or if the stock settles over or at the higher strike call.

This technique has both the limited downside and limited upside.

CALL AND PUT OPTIONS EXAMPLES AND DEFINITIONS

Call and put options are subsidiary investments, which implies their value developments rely upon the price or value movements of another money-related item, which is normally called the underlying.

- A call option is purchased if the dealer expects the price of the underlying should ascend within a specific period

- A put option is purchased if the dealer expects the underlying to fall within a specific period.

Puts and calls can likewise be written/sold, which generates pay, be that as it may, it gives specific rights to the buyer of the option.

Breaking Down the Call Option

For the United States - style options, a call is an options contract that gives the purchaser the option to purchase the underlying assets at a set cost at any time up to the termination date, popularly called the expiration date. Purchasers of European-style options may practice the option—purchase the underlying—just on the termination date.

Strike Price

The strike price is the foreordained cost at which a call purchaser can purchase the underlying asset. For example, the buyer of a stock call option with a strike cost of 10 can use the option to buy that stock at 10USD before the option lapses.

Options lapse/expiration change and can be short term or long term. It is advisable for the call buyer to practice their option, and require the call writer or seller to sell them the stock at the strike price, if the current expense of the underlying is above the strike cost. For instance, if the stock is trading at $9 on the stock market, it isn't beneficial for the call option purchaser to practice their option to purchase the stock at $10 because they can get it at a lower cost on the market.

What the Call Buyer Gets

The call purchaser has the privilege to purchase a stock at the strike price for several times. For that right, the call purchaser pays a premium. In the event that the price of the underlying moves over the strike value, the option will be worth money, which means it will have intrinsic value.

The purchaser can sell the option for a profit (this is what that most call purchasers do) or practice the option at expiry (get the shares).

What the Call Seller Gets

The call seller/writer gets the premium. Writing call options is an approach to generate income. Be that as it may, the income from composing a call option is constrained to the premium, while a call purchaser has hypothetically boundless profit potential.

Computing the Call Option's Cost

One stock call option contract represents a hundred shares of the underlying stock. Stock call costs are commonly quoted per share. Thusly, ascertain how much buying the agreement will cost, take the expense of the option, and multiply it by 100.

Call options can be out of, in or in, at money.

- In the money means that the underlying asset cost is over the call strike cost.
- Out of the money implies the underlying price is beneath the strike price.
- At the money implies the underlying cost and the strike price are the same.

You can purchase a call in any of those three stages. Your premium will be bigger for an in the money option since it as of now has inherent value.

Breaking Down the Put Option

For the United States - style options, a put is an options contract that gives the purchaser the option to sell the underlying asset at a set cost at any time up to the lapse date (expiration date). Purchasers of European-style options may practice the option—sell the underlying—just on the expiration date.

Strike Price

The strike price is the foreordained cost at which a put purchaser can sell the underlying asset. For instance, the purchaser of a stock put option with a strike price of $10 can utilize the option to sell that stock at $10 before the option lapses or expires. It is prudent for the put buyer to rehearse their option, and need the put seller to buy the stock from them at the strike cost, just if the current cost of the underlying is underneath the strike cost.

For instance, if the stock is trading at $11 on the stock market, it isn't beneficial for the put option purchaser to practice their option to sell the stock at $10 because they can sell it at a greater price on the market.

What the Put Buyer Gets

The put purchaser has the privilege to sell a stock at the strike price several times. For that right, the put purchaser pays a premium. If the cost of the underlying moves underneath the strike price, the option will be worth money (will have inherent value). The purchaser can sell the option for a profit (what most put purchasers do) or practice the option at expiry (i.e sell the shares).

What the Put Seller Gets

The put seller/writer gets the premium. Composing put options is an approach to generate income, Be that as it may, the income from composing a put option is restricted to the premium, while a put purchaser's maximum profit potential happens if the stock goes to zero.

Computing the Put Option's Cost

Put contracts signify 100 shares of the basic stock, much the same as call option contracts. To find the cost of the contract, multiply the underlying share price cost by 100.

Put options can be in, at, or out of the money, much the same as call options.

- In the money implies the underlying asset cost is underneath the put strike price.
- Out of the money implies the underlying cost is over the strike price.
- At the money implies the underlying cost and the strike price are the same.

Also with a call option, you can purchase a put option in any of those three stages. Your premium will be bigger for an in the money option because it already has inherent value.

Chapter 10:
ROLLING OPTIONS OUT, UP, AND DOWN

E ach option trading situation is unique. Once in awhile, you'll purchase a call option, nail the directional move 100 percent, and leave the strategy a major victor upon expiration. However, sometime, your position may require some tweaking to accomplish its most extreme potential. Here, we'll talk about various strategies for rolling options, whether you're hoping to alter your position out, down, or up.

Rolling Out

"Rolling out" implies that an expiring option position is being supplanted with an indistinguishable trade in a later options arrangement. For instance, you may sell to close a January 50 call, and all the while purchase to open a March 50 call.

There are two situations where it bodes well to roll out. In the first, you have pinpointed a triumphant options procedure, and you feel certain that the directional move will keep on playing out in your favor. By taking profits on the shorter-term trade and at the same time starting the more extended term trade, you are positioned to continue picking up from a drawn-out move in your favor.

In the second, you still feel assured in your unique expectation for the stock - however, you've concluded that additional time is fundamental for the trade to play out as you anticipate. In this situation, you're purchasing more time for the shares to satisfy your expectations.

In the two cases, rolling out ought to be approached with alert. Under the main situation, be sure that the outlook for the stock keeps on supporting your trade theory, and that you are not just getting avaricious after a healthy winner. In the subsequent model, again - reevaluate your rationale for the trade. Does the stock essentially need a couple of more weeks to move in your favor, or is it an opportunity to concede that your underlying analysis may have been misguided?

Rolling Up

"Rolling up" means that you're trading out lower-strike options for contracts with a higher strike price. If you have played a considered option and the stock makes a snappy, sensational move in your favor, rolling up is an approach to raise the bullish stakes: you sell to close your current call option at a profit and purchase to open a higher-strike call for (in a perfect world) a little measure of capital. Along these lines, you've secured some profits on your first trade exchange, and you've also procured some new influence to profit from a proceeded move higher.

You may likewise choose to roll up if you have written a covered call, and the stock has made a move higher that puts you at risk of a potential task. The current short option will be purchased to close, while a higher-strike call will be sold to open. In the most ideal situation, the credits gotten (from the sold calls at both the rolled-up strike and the first strike) will be adequate to offset your purchase to-close expenses and any extra brokerage charges and commissions.

These are only a couple of models, as there are different situations where rolling up may also bode well. For instance, in case you're selling puts on stock to bet on specialized help, and the stock has transcended your chosen strike, you may roll up to gather a higher premium.

Rolling Down

"Rolling down" includes the closeout of a higher-strike option in return for a lower-strike option. Inverting the model above, you may decide to roll down on the off chance that you've bought put options that returned huge gains in your favor of you soon after they were started. By selling to close the in-the-money options and trading them for less expensive puts at a lower strike, you can profit by a proceeded move lower by the shares.

On the other hand, you may roll down a short call position if the underlying stock is slanting lower, or roll down a short put if the stock is dropping and you would like to keep away from a task.

One Final Note

Any of the above strategies for rolling options can be consolidated to suit your necessities. For instance, if you'd prefer to broaden a winning call trade, you may decide to roll the option up and out, choosing both a higher strike and a longer-dated arrangement.

As shown above, however, be certain that you're not moving options to hinder an unavoidable loss. If a trade is moving immovably against you, it's frequently best to just finish off the position and take your lumps. Else, you risk piling on extra transaction fees - and possibly more losses.

Chapter 11:
CREDIT AND DEBIT SPREAD

Whentrading or investing in options, there are a few option spread techniques that one could utilize—a spread being the buy and offer of various options on a similar underlying as a bundle.

While we can characterize spreads in different manners, one regular dimension is to ask whether or not the technique is a debit spread or a charge spread. Net credit spreads, credit spreads are spread strategy that includes net receipts of premiums, however, debit spreads include net payment of premiums.

KEY TAKEAWAYS

- An option spread is a method that incorporates the simultaneous buying and selling of options on the same fundamental asset.
- A credit spread incorporates selling a high-premium option while purchasing a low-premium option in a comparative class or of comparative security, resulting in a credit to the dealer's account.
- A debit spread involves buying a high-premium option while selling a low-premium option in a similar class or of similar security, resulting in a charge from the merchant's account.

Credit Spreads

A credit spread involves writing, or selling, a high-premium option, and at the same time purchasing a lower premium option. The premium got from the writing option is more prominent than the premium paid for the long option, resulting in a premium credited into the investor or trader's account when the position is opened. At the point when investors or traders utilize a credit spread technique, the most extreme profit they get is the net premium. The credit spread results in a profit when the options narrow.

For instance, a merchant actualizes a credit spread technique by writing in one March call option with a strike price of $30 for $3 and all the while buying one March call option at $40 for $1. Since the typical multiplier on a value option is 100, the net premium got is $200 for the trade. Moreover, the merchant will benefit if the spread strategy narrows.

A bearish broker expects that stock costs should diminish, and, along these lines, purchases call options (long call) at a specific strike price and sells (short call) a similar number of call options within the same class and with the same lapse at a lower strike price. Interestingly, bullish traders anticipate that stock costs should rise, and in this way, purchase call options at a specific strike price and sell the same number of call options within a similar class and with a similar expiration at a higher strike price.

Debit Spreads

A debit spread—regularly utilized by novices to options strategies—includes purchasing an option with a higher premium and at the same time selling an option with a lower premium, where the premium paid for the long option of the spread is more than the premium received from the composed option.

A debit spread results in a premium fee, or paid, from the trader's or investor's account when the position is opened. Debit spreads are used to balance the costs related to claiming long options positions.

For instance, a broker purchases one May put option with a strike price of $20 for $5 and at the same time sells one May put option with a strike price of $10 for $1. Consequently, he paid $4, or $400 for the trade. On the off chance that the trade is out of the money, his maximum loss is decreased to $400, instead of $500 if he just purchased the put option.

Credit or Debit Options Spreads? How Do You Choose?

Some decisions are simple, similar to how you put your pants on. In addition to the fact that you are most likely to go with the one-leg-at-a-time, fly-in-the-front strategy, but at the same time it's the conspicuous decision. If you trade options, in addition to the fact that you need to know whether you think a stock will go up or down, you also need to think about volatility (vol), as well. Is it low or high? Will it go down or up from here? This is where traders get hung up on methodology. When you have the information you need, which options spread do you run with? Is there an approach to computerize the decision-making process? Maybe.

Vertical spreads specifically are guilty of overwhelming even the best of them. A vertical spread is a characterized-risk strategy that lets you make bearish or bullish theoretical trades. Also, they are flexible. You can make a vertical with a lot of risks or minimize risk. A vertical could be a momentary hypothesis or long haul directional play.

So Many Ways to Trade 'Em

Vertical spreads are clear. They're made out of either a short and long call or a long and short put in the same expiration. Keep in mind, if we're discussing bullish verticals, the two choices are short put verticals for credit or long call verticals for debit. If we're discussing bearish verticals, your choice is short call verticals for a credit or long put verticals for a debit. Which one is which? Utilize the cheat sheet.

Chapter 12:
COMMON OPTIONS TRADING MISTAKES TO AVOID

L earn about the most widely recognized options trading mistakes so you can settle on more informed trading choices.

As a new options merchant, it isn't remarkable to feel overpowered. One of the advantages of trading options is that it gives you an assortment of approaches to take advantage of what you accept may happen to the underlying security. In any case, one of the trade-offs for the luxury of this assortment is an expanded risk for committing errors. This part of the book is to create awareness in regards to the most common options trading mistakes to help options traders settle on more informed choices.

#1: Strategy doesn't match your outlook

A significant component when starting to trade options is the ability to build up an outlook for what you believe could occur. Two of the regular beginning stages for building up an outlook are utilizing fundamental analysis and technical analysis, or a combination of both. The technical analysis revolves around deciphering market activity (mainly price and volume) on a graph and searching for regions of resistance, support, and trends to distinguish potential purchase/sell opportunities. The fundamental analysis incorporates inspecting an organization's performance data, financial statements, and current business trends to formulate an outlook on the organization's worth. An outlook not only comprises a directional inclination, however it entails a time frame for how long you believe your idea will take to work.

As you survey various options techniques, it is critical to ensure the strategy you pick is intended to take advantage of the outlook you expect. Fidelity's Options Strategy Guide is one approach to acclimate yourself with various methodologies and can assist you in determining the most appropriate one for your circumstance.

#2: Choosing the wrong expiration

Likewise, with strategies, you are confronted with the issue of having a multitude of decisions when choosing an expiration date. Fortunately, if you build up an outlook, at that point choosing the right expiration generally falls into place. One way to assist you with picking the best expiration for your outlook is to have a simple agenda:

- How long do I believe it will take for the exchange/trade to play out?
- Do I need to hold the trade through a profit declaration, stock split, or other events?
- Is there sufficient liquidity to help my trade?

#3: Choosing an inappropriate position size

The most position measuring errors originate from two common emotions: greed or fear. If you are greedy when deciding, you could wind up trading a position size that is unreasonably enormous for your account size. This may happen when a trade conflicts with the outlook and afterward you're left with a devastating loss. Then again, you could be like a few traders who trade very little. Trading a little size is fine, however, you may pass up a material return.

Regular ways of position sizing include:

- Risk a percentage of your account value
  - 1%, 2%, 3%, etc.
- Use a predictable dollar value
  - $100, $500, $1,000, etc.

Eventually, when settling on the trade size, you ought to be comfortable with the sum of capital you will lose if the trade does not go in your favor. In a perfect world, the trade size ought to be sufficiently enormous to be meaningful to the account, but little enough so you do not lose sleep at night.

#4: Ignoring volatility

Implied volatility is a proportion of what the market anticipates that volatility should be in the future for given security. It is critical to perceive whenever implied volatility is generally high or low because it helps to determine the cost of the option premium. Knowing whether the premium is costly or modest is a significant factor when settling on what option methodology bodes well for your outlook. If the options are moderately modest, it might be smarter to take a look at debit techniques, though if the options are generally costly, you might be better off searching for credit strategies.

#5: Not using probability

Considering the probabilities for your strategy is a significant factor when deciding to place a trade. Not only does it puts into consideration what is measurably prone to occur, however, it is basic to comprehension if your reward/risk bodes well. Note that probability has no directional inclination. It is essentially the factual possibility of price being at a specific level on the assessment date, given the present components. You can utilize Fidelity's Probability Calculator (provided by Dash Financial Technologies LLC) to help make this determination.

#6: Focusing on the expiration graph

As a merchant, it is essential to continually evaluate the amount of reward/risk you have on the table and verify whether it still bodes well for your account. Solely concentrating on your positions expiration diagram doesn't tell how much risk you carry today, or on a future date.

Utilizing the Profit/Loss Calculator device (provided by Dash Financial Technologies LLC) can assist you with perceiving how your position will respond to price movements today and any other day in the future until expiration.

Mistake #7: Not having a trading plan

One of the initial phases in avoiding basic trading errors is to have a sound trading plan. An essential trading plan should comprise of, however not be constrained to:

- How much are you ready to risk per trade?
- How will you discover opportunities in the market?
- When will you enter the trade?
- What is your exit technique?

As referenced previously, greed and fear can prompt nonsensical choices that you wouldn't ordinarily make. The principle advantage of having a trading plan is to expel these emotional feelings from your trading. It likewise makes an effectively repeatable procedure. Repeatability is a significant factor to assist you with learning from mistakes and can see mistakes in the trade you place. Without an arrangement, it turns out to be hard to improve as a merchant and continue pushing forward.

Trading options involve various contemplations both when the trade has been set. A large number of the errors referenced can be represented before the trade is opened by using the devices and assets Fidelity offers. The absolute most significant advance to trading options is to build up a plan and stick with it! A portion of the devices and assets that can assist you with building up your arrangement incorporates the Options Strategy Guide, Probability Calculator, Key Statistics, and the Profit/Loss Calculator. Take advantage of these and other trading apparatuses and assets Fidelity provides to assist you with maintaining a strategic distance from these regular options trading mistakes in your future trades.

Chapter 13:
BENEFITS AND RISKS OF TRADING OPTIONS

Ptions offer investors more financial and strategic advantage than they can get by basically purchasing, selling, or shorting stocks. Traders can utilize options to secure against portfolio losses, catch a stock for less than it sells on the open market or sells it for more, increment the profit on a current or new position, and reduces the risk on theoretical bets in a wide range of economic situations.

Indeed, there are a lot of encouraging points in the advantages vs disadvantages of options trading. However, there likewise are intrinsic risks. Here are a few things each potential options dealer ought to consider.

The advantages of trading options

It necessitates a lower upfront financial commitment than stock trading. The cost of purchasing an option (the premium in addition to the trading commission) is lesser than what an investor would need to pay to buy shares inside and out.

The options traders/investors pay less out-of-money to play in a similar sandbox, however, if the trades go their direction they'll profit just as much as the investor who dished out for the stock.

There's a restricted drawback for option purchasers.
At the point when you purchase a call or put option, you aren't
committed to following through on the trade. If your
expectations about the period and direction of a stock's
trajectory are off base, your losses are constrained to whatever
you paid for the trading fees and contract. However, the
drawback can be a lot more prominent for options sellers — see
the downsides segment below.

Options offer implicit flexibility for traders. Before an
options contract terminates, investors have a few vital moves
they can deploy. These moves include:

- Exercise the option and purchase the shares to add to their
  portfolio
- Exercise the option, purchase the offers and afterward sell
  a few or every one of them
- Sell the "in the money" options agreement/contract to
  another investor
- Potentially make back a portion of the money spent on an
  "out of the money" option by selling the
  agreement/contract to another investor before it
  terminates

Options empower an investor to fix a stock cost. In an
action like putting something on loan, options contracts allow
investors to freeze the stock cost at a specific amount (the strike
price) for a particular timeframe. Contingent upon the sort of
option utilized, it ensures that investors will have the option to
purchase or sell the stock at the strike price whenever before
the option contract terminates.

THE DRAWBACKS OF TRADING OPTIONS

Options expose dealers to boundless/intensified losses. In contrast to an option purchaser (or holder), the option seller can incur losses a lot more prominent than the cost of the agreement/contract. Keep in mind, when an investor writes call or put, the person in question is committed to purchase or sell shares at a predetermined cost inside the contracts period, regardless of whether the cost is unfavorable (and there's no cap on how high a stock cost can rise).

There's restricted time for the investing postulation to bear out. The idea of options is short term. Options dealers and investors are hoping to benefit from a close term value development, which must happen within days, weeks, or months for the contract/trade to pay off. That requires making two right presumptions: picking the proper time to purchase the option agreement/contract, and choosing precisely when to exercise, sell or leave before the option terminates. Long haul stock investors aren't on a cutoff time. They have time — years, in fact, decades — to let their investing proposals play out.

Potential traders must meet certain prerequisites. Before you can even begin trading options, you should apply for endorsement through your broker. After responding to a progression of inquiries concerning your financial means, investing experience, and comprehension of the intrinsic risks of options trading, the dealer will relegate you a trading level that directs what sorts of options trades you're permitted to place. Any investor who trades options must keep at least $2,000 in their investment fund, which is an industry necessity and an opportunity cost worth considering.

Options investors may incur extra costs that influence their profit and loss results. A few options trading techniques, (for example, selling call options on securities you do not possess) require investors to set up a margin account — which essentially is a credit extension that fills in as collateral in case the trade moves against the investor. Every financier firm has distinctive minimum requirements for creating an margin account and will base the sum and interest rate on how much money and protections are in the account. Margin loan fees regularly can go from the low single digits to the low twofold digits.

If an investor can't follow through on the loan (or if the brokerage fund balance plunges beneath a specific rate, as can occur because of daily market variances), the lender can give a margin call and sell an investor's account if the investor question doesn't add more money or stocks to it.

The Options Clearing Corporation gives a nitty-gritty summary of the qualities and risks of normalized options and a review of U.S. government income tax rules that influence those putting resources into options and other monetary items.

Other considerations

To conclude whether to purchase, sell, or hold a stock as long as possible, you should know the organization's business back to front and have a clear sense of which course the asset is going. Options investors should be hyper-mindful of these things.

Options achievement requires investors to have a decent handle of the organization's intrinsic value, but maybe even above all, they likewise need to have a strong proposal about ways the business has been and will be influenced by close term factors, for example, macroeconomic effects, internal operations, and the sector/competition.

A lot of investors may conclude that options add unnecessary unpredictability to their financial lives. However, in case you're keen on investigating the opportunities that options brings to the table — and have the constitution and the money to withstand potential losses — this book will can help limit your drawback.

Chapter 14:
STOCK MARKET

The stock market is the place you can purchase, sell, and trade stocks any business day. It's likewise called a stock trade.

Stocks permit you to claim a share of a public corporation. The stock cost depends on the corporation's earnings. If the organization does well, or regardless of whether everybody thinks the organization is going nicely, the stock cost goes up. Stocks likewise rise when the economy does well. Many organizations likewise give a dividend payment every year to the stockholder, which gives additional extra value.

Why Companies Sell Stocks

Organizations sell stocks to get the brokers to grow bigger. At the point when individuals need to begin a business, they frequently pay for it with individual loans or even their credit cards. When they develop the organization enough, they can get bank loans. They can also sell bonds to individual investors.

In the end, they'll need a great deal of cash to take the business to the following stage. Around then, they will sell the main stocks, called an initial public offering. When that occurs, no single individual owns the organization since they have sold it to the stockholders. Since the U.S. stock market is so modern, it is simpler in this nation than in many others to take a company public. It enables the economy to extend since it gives a lift up to companies wishing to grow very huge.

The requirement for organizations to raise money, and investors to profit from them, is what keeps the stock market up.

Why Invest in the Stock Market

Stock market investing is the most ideal approach to accomplish returns that beat inflation over time. There are four different advantages of investing.

Stock ownership exploits a developing economy.

Unlike brokers, it's anything but difficult to purchase stocks and just as simple to sell.

The best part is that you can make money in two different ways. A few investors like to let their stock appreciate over time.

Others favor stocks that deliver dividends to give a consistent income stream.

There are seven different ways for you to invest in the stock market. The quickest and least expensive is to buy them online. If you need more direction at a sensible value, join an investment club. A full-service broker will cost all the more however could Value the price. The person will give you proficient suggestions. A money manager charges the most yet will accomplish all the work for you.

Rather than purchasing singular stocks, you could get them as part of an index fund or mutual fund. An index fund follows an index, for example, the MSCI developing market index. A mutual fund has a manager that purchases the stocks for you.

The most dangerous is the hedge fund. They likewise invest in derivatives, which could build the return but will also increase the risk.

Investing Risks

The most noteValuey downside is that you can lose your whole investment if the stock value falls to zero. If the organization goes bankrupt, stock investors are paid after bondholders. Thus, stock investing can be an emotional rollercoaster. If you need guaranteed returns, stick to bonds. Be that as it may, if you are in it as long as possible, stocks are a superior approach.

At the point when stock market costs decay under 10%, that is known as a stock market revision. At the point when costs fall that much or more in one day, it's known as a stock market crash. At the point when costs fall 20% or more, it's known as a bear advertise. These usually last 18 months. The inverse is a bull market, and they last two to five years.

The U.S. Stock market Is the World's Financial Capital

The United States in the area of the two biggest trades on the planet. The New York Stock Trade accounts for 2,400 organizations. They are Value around $21 trillion in market capitalization. That is the estimation of all of its offers. The NYSE is arranged on Wall Street. The Nasdaq has 3,800 company with a market top of $11 trillion. It's arranged in Times Square. Both are in Manhattan, New York.

The stock market works by coordinating buyers and dealers. The two significant trades do it any other way from one another. The NYSE is a genuine auction house. It coordinates the most noteValuey offer at the least sales price. There is a market producer for each stock who will fill in the hole to guarantee exchanges go without any problem. At the Nasdaq, purchasers and merchants exchange with a seller as opposed to each other. It's done electronically, so exchanges happen in split seconds.

The United States is the world's monetary capital since its financial markets are so advanced. Therefore, as a result, information on companies is easy to obtain. This transparency builds the trust of investors from around the globe. Thus, the U.S. stock market draws in more investors. That makes it much simpler for a U.S. organization to open up to the world.

The presentation of the general U.S. stock market is followed by its three head accounts: the Dow Jones Industrial Average, the S&P 500, and the Nasdaq. Various parts of the markets are likewise followed. For instance, the MSCI Index tracks the presentation of stocks in developing market countries, for example, China, India, and Brazil.

Major World Stock Markets

Each significant nation has a stock trade. Here are the best 10, positioned by total market capitalization. They are accounted with the most quoted indices that are nearest to estimating their performances:

- New York Stock Trade - NYSE
- Nasdaq - The trade likewise has an account by a similar name.
- Tokyo Stock Trade - Nikkei 225.
- London Stock Trade - FTSE 100

- Euronext - Euronext 100. Other European files are the AEX (Amsterdam), BEL (Brussels), CAC (Paris), DAX (Germany), and PSI (Lisbon).
- Shanghai Stock Trade - Shanghai Stock Trade
- Hong Kong Stock Trade - Hang Seng.
- Toronto Stock Trade - SPTSX.
- Bombay Stock Trade - SENSEX.
- National Stock Trade of India - NSE Nifty.
- BM&F Bovespa (Brazil) - The file is additionally called BOVESPA.

Other Financial Markets

The stock market is only one type of financial market. Before you invest, ensure you know about them all:

Items are generally traded in future options, which make them increasingly confounded. They incorporate grains, oil, and the abnormally named pork bellies.

Foreign trade is the place individuals purchase and sell currencies. It's high risk because the qualities can change drastically for no evident explanation and change rapidly.

Derivatives are exceptionally complicated bonds that get their incentive from the hidden resource, for example, subprime mortgages. Singular investors should remain away. Although they can offer huge returns, they can likewise offer huge returns, they can also deplete your entire life savings in a day.

Supply and Demand

Stock costs are an element of supply and demand, although other influences—such as earnings and the economy might affect the desirability of owning or selling a specific stock. If an organization reports shockingly low profit, demand for its stock may fade, and as the value drops, the harmony among buyers and sellers is changed. Buyers will begin mentioning discount off the present cost and many prodded sellers will oblige them to dispose of the stocks. When there are a larger number of sellers than there are buyers, this makes more supply than demand, so the value starts to fall.

The Role of Prices

Eventually, a stock's cost may drop to a level where buyers find it attractive, or some other factor will change the dynamic. As buyers move into the market, demand turns out to be quicker than supply, and the expense correspondingly goes up. Sometimes supply and demand discover a balance—a value that purchasers acknowledge and that seller oblige. Costs will bounce up and down when market supply and demand are generally equivalent, yet they will do it in a narrow price range. It's workable for a stock to remain in this range for a considerable length of time or even a very long time before another outside factor disturbs the supply and demand balance and causes either a perceptible increase or decrease in cost.

If interest for a stock surpasses the supply, its cost will rise, yet it will just increment to a point where buyers speculate that demand is disappearing. By then, holders of the stock will probably start selling. Some may have ridden the cost up and accept an inversion is coming, so they sell their shares and take their benefits while they are still ahead.

At the point when stock costs start to fall—which can occur for a few reasons—and more owners begin selling their shares, there will be more supply than there is demand. To tempt buyers, sellers must drop costs to oblige for the saturated market. A similar unique deals with the opposite side, however in a switch. As the value falls, it will arrive at a level that buyers find attractive. As buyers get shares, the stock's cost will rise because sellers must be lured to let go of their shares.

Understanding stock market fluctuations

It is surely known that the stock market is unstable and hard to anticipate. What is less well understood is why. What are the raw sources of economic factors that drive these sporadic changes? By a long shot the majority of the discourse in the press, additionally most economic hypotheses, declares that the market is driven by shocks (erratic variances) to macroeconomic basics that have significant consequences for economic growth. We argue here, notwithstanding, that the most significant irregular powers behind the more drawn out term gains in the US stock exchange have not been drivers of financial development, however, have rather been an aggregation of irregular shocks – to a great extent uncorrelated with economic development that have brought about redistribution among laborers and investors.

The irregular shocks behind the instability and unpredictability of the market ought not to be conflated with purely deterministic long term trends. There is little puzzle that the genuine estimation of the stock market floats upward over significant stretches in a to a great extent unsurprising path as efficiency (driven by innovative advancement) improves. This same deterministic pattern has likewise pushed yield per capita and the average way of life upward in the course of the last several centuries. It is rather the random shocks, the bloom and busts around this trend, about which we have little information, yet on which a continuous stream of media theory centers. Such random shocks can steadily displace the market from its long term pattern for periods up to quite a few years. What drives these movements in the market?

Early evidence recommended that one source of such irregular fluctuations is countercyclical assortment in the stock exchange risk premium(e.g., Fama and French 1989)however was quiet on its sources, also the sources of cash flow risk that have little to do with the market risk premium yet nonetheless can have large effects on the stock value level. Hence the question remains, what are the sources of stochastic fluctuation that drive the market?

Clarifying developments in stock riches

Our examination begins with an experimental investigation, prodded by a simple accounting exercise. Consider a firm that produces yield, offers it to make benefit, at that point divide those income between compensation delivered to laborers and profits paid to investors. We refer to workers' and investors' segments of salary as 'factor shares'. The estimation of a part of stock in this firm, which is a case on the company's present and future profits, can increment for a mix of three in a general sense random reasons:

- The firm becomes more productive, producing more earnings and subsequently higher dividends, while factor shares remain fixed.
- The firm decreases the shares of earnings going to workers, consequently expanding the part got by shareholders as dividends, while total income stays fixed.
- Earnings nor factor shares change, yet investors become more willing to hold the stock for some other reason (e.g., changes in chance resilience).

To measure the effectiveness of these three types of movements over time, we estimate a cointegrated vector autoregression (VAR) of utilization, work pay, and asset wealth (all in genuine, log per capita terms). We decompose the residuals of the VAR into three commonly symmetrical parts identifying with the three sorts of developments depicted previously:

A disturbance that affects utilization, work pay, and resource riches on impact, which might be interpreted as a shock to production technology.

- A disturbance that moves work pay one way and resource riches in the other while leaving aggregate(worker plus shareholder) utilization unaltered on impact, which might be interpreted as a shock to factor shares.
- A disturbance that influences only resource wealth on impact, leaving utilization and labor income unchanged, which may be interpreted as a shock to investors' ability to hold risky bonds that is unrelated to current economic activity.

Figure 1. VAR motivation reactions

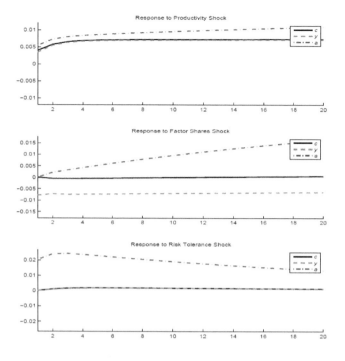

Figure 1 shows dynamic reactions in US data. The productive technology shock expands utilization, asset wealth, and work salary by similar amounts, steady with an expansion in overall output. The factor share shock increases assets wealth while decreasing work pay and leaving consumption fixed, consistent with capital owners getting a bigger share of an unaltered pie. That consumption stays fixed on impact is an identifying assumption. A significant empirical result is that the subsequent reaction of consumption is essentially zero. Hence, the components share stock is simply redistributive, it doesn't forecast any expansion in the total pie anytime not far off. The risk resilience shock influences just asset costs, steady with an adjustment in investor preferences separated from changes in the genuine economy. As in the past, the zero contemporaneous reactions of consumption and work pay to this stock are distinguishing assumptions, however the finding that these factors never show huge reactions even subsequently is a result, suggesting that the risk tolerance shock is disconnected from traditional macroeconomic activity.

Up until this point, our investigation has consolidated a wide range of family unit riches as resource riches. To draw out the implications of these exact unsettling influences for the stock exchange (a section of family unit riches), we next take changes in stock riches and relapse them on current and loosened symmetrical zed VAR aggravations. We find that these shocks explain by a long shot generally (87%) of changes in quarterly stock wealth development, suggesting that we can decompose practically the entirety of the variety in the US stock exchange into segments relating to these three sources of economic variation. We find that:

At the point when we measure variety in the stock market over short to intermediate horizons (for example over months, quarters, and business cycle frequencies), fluctuations in stock market development are ruled by shocks to risk tolerance that have no noticeable impact on the genuine economy.

Over longer skylines (i.e., over decades), 40-half of the variety in stock riches development can be credited to factors share shocks - those that move the stock exchange one way and work pay in the other.

Shocks to gainful innovation have a little impact on fluctuations in stock costs at all horizons.

This investigation likewise permits us to break down historical movements in stock wealth.

Figure 2. Level deterioration (Data)

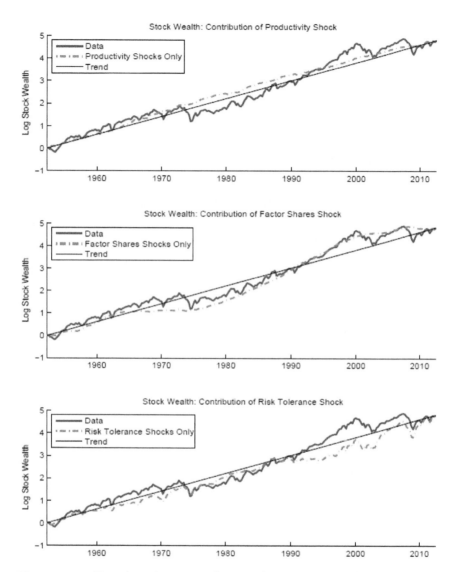

The strong line in Figure 2 shows the post-war deterministic pattern. The three shocks displace the market from this example. Here, the most striking component is the big swings in stock exchange wealth around designs that have been inferable from developments in factor shares (center board), which has incited a sharp rise in stock riches since the late 1970s. For example of the size of these powers for the long-run advancement of the stock exchange, we break down the percent change since 1980 in the deterministically genuine estimation of stock exchange riches that is owing to each shock. The period since 1980 is an interesting one to consider, as the all-out effect of the factor shares stocks tenaciously redistributed rewards from workers and toward investors. (The converse was substantial from the mid-1960s to mid-1980s.) We discover that if there had been no such reallocation since 1980, the level of the stock exchange would be commonly 50% of its Value today. Besides, the model works excellent job of explaining the long-run developments in the market; together, the three commonly orthogonal economic shocks we identify explain almost all of the increase in detrended genuine stock market wealth since 1980 (explicitly, they represent 110% of the increment, with the remaining - 10%accounted for by a residual). These discoveries imply that the irregular shocks answerable for greatest developments in stock market wealth over the last 30 years are not those that raise or lower aggregate rewards, yet are rather ones that redistribute a given degree of level of rewards between workers and shareholders.

The Major Types of Risks for Stock Investors

Investing comes with risks, yet thoughtful investment determinations that meet your objectives and risk profile keep individual stock and bond risks at an adequate level. However, other risks you have no power over are inherent in investing. Most of these risks influence the market or economy and require investors to change portfolios or ride out the storm.

Here are four significant kinds of risks that investors face, alongside some strategies for dealing with the issues brought about by these market and economic shifts.

Economic Risk

One of the most evident risks of investing is that the economy can turn sour at some random second. Following the market collapse in 2000 and terrorist attacks on September 11, 2001, the economy died down into a harsh spell, and a mix of elements saw the market index lose critical rates. It returned quite a while to come to levels close September 11 marks, just to have the bottom fall out again in the 2008 money related crisis.

For youthful investors, the best technique is frequently to hunker down and ride out these downturns. If you can build your situation in great strong organizations, these troughs are normally acceptable occasions to do as such. Foreign stocks can be a splendid spot when domestic market is in the dumps, and big thanks to globalization, several U.S. associations increase a larger part of their advantages abroad. In any case, in a collapse like the 2008 financial crisis, there might be no safe places to turn.

More established investors are stuck in a more tightly tough situation. If you are in or close to retirement, a significant downturn in the stock market can be destroyed if you haven't moved critical assets for bonds or fixed-income bonds. This is the reason broadening in your portfolio is fundamental.

Inflationary Risk

Inflation is the tax on everybody, and if it's too high, it can destroy value and create recessions. Although we believe inflation is heavily influenced by us, the cure of higher interest rates may, eventually, be as awful as the issue. With the massive government acquiring to fund the improvement bundles, it is just a short time before inflation returns.[2]

Investors have historically retreated to hard assets, for example, brokers and precious metals, particularly gold, during inflation, since they're probably going to withstand the change. Inflation harms investors on fixed salaries the most since it breaks down the estimation of their pay stream. Stocks are the best security against inflation since associations can alter cost to the rate of inflation. A worldwide recession may mean stocks will battle for an extended amount of time before the economy is strong enough to bear higher prices. It's anything but an ideal arrangement, yet that is the reason even resigned investors ought to keep up a assets in stocks.

Market Value Risk

Market esteem chance refers to what happens when the market turns or disregards your investment. It happens when the market goes off chasing the "following hot thing" and leaves some extraordinary, anyway unexciting organizations behind. It additionally happens when the market collapses since great stocks, just as bad stocks, endure as investors rush out of the market.

A few investors find this a good thing and view it as an opportunity to load up on great stocks when the market isn't bidding down the cost. Then again, it doesn't propel your motivation to watch your investments flatline month after month while different parts of the market are going up.

Try not to get caught with all your investments in a single part of the economy. By spreading your investments over a few divisions, you have a superior possibility of taking an interest in the development of some of your stocks at any one time.

Risk of Being Too Conservative

There is nothing wrong with being a conservative or careful investor. However, if you never face any challenges, it might be difficult to show up at your financial objectives. You may need to back 15–20 years of retirement with your retirement reserve, and keeping it all in low-intrigue investment funds instruments may not take care of business. Younger investors should be increasingly aggressive with their portfolios, as they have the opportunity to bounce back if the market turns terrible.

Market Timing

Market timing is the procedure of choosing buying or selling decisions of money related resources (regularly stocks) by endeavoring to anticipate future market value developments. The prediction may be founded on a outlook of market or economic conditions coming about because of fundamental or technical analysis. This is an investment procedure dependent on the outlook for a total market, rather than for a particular money related resource.

Whether market timing is ever a feasible investment technique is controversial. Some may consider showcase timing to be a form of gambling dependent on pure possibility, since they don't put stock in underestimated or exaggerated markets. The productive market theory asserts that financial costs consistently show irregular walk behavior and subsequently can't be predicted with consistency. Some consider market timing to be reasonable in specific situations, for example, a clear air pocket. Notwithstanding, because the economy is a complex system that contains many elements, even on the occasion of significant market optimism or negativity, it stays difficult, if certainly feasible, to predetermine the local maximum or minimum of future costs with any accuracy; a supposed bubble can keep going at many years before costs collapse. Similarly, an accident can continue for expanded periods; stocks that appear to be "cheap" initially can regularly turn out to be a lot less expensive a short time later, before then either rebounding at some time in the future or heading toward bankruptcy for chapter 11. Proponents of market timing counter that market timing is simply one more name for trading. They contend that "endeavoring to predict future market value developments" is the thing that all traders do, whether or not they trade individual stocks or a variety of stocks, otherwise known as, mutual fund. Hence if market timing is certifiably not a reasonable investment system, the proponents say, then neither is any of the trading on the various stock trades. The individuals who disagree with this view normally advocate a buy-and-hold strategy with periodic "re-balancing". Others battle that predicting the next event that will influence the economy and stock costs is notoriously difficult.

What is Timing Risk

Timing risk is the theory that investor goes into when attempting to buy or sell a stock based on future price predictions. Timing risk clarifies the potential for missing up valuable developments in cost because of a blunder in timing. This could make hurt the value of an investor's portfolio resulting from purchasing too high or selling excessively low.

Separating Timing Risk

There is some discussion about the feasibility of timing. Some express that it's difficult to time the market reliably; others state that market timing is the way to better than average returns. A predominant idea regarding this matter is that it is smarter to have "time in the market" than endeavoring to "time the market." The development of financial markets after some time underpins this, as does the way that many dynamic administrators neglect to beat market averages after considering in exchange costs.

For instance, an investor is presented to timing risk if he anticipates a market remedy and chooses to trade his whole portfolio in the desire for repurchasing the stocks back at a lower cost. The investor risks the opportunity of the stocks expanding before he buys in.

Timing Risk and Performance

A study analyzing investor behavior found that, during the October 2014 downturn, one out of five investors diminished exposure to stocks, trade traded assets (ETFs) and mutual fund, and generally 1% of investors decreased their portfolios by 90% or more.

Further analysis found that investors who sold most of their portfolios had significantly underperformed the investors who took little or zero move during the revision. The investors who sold 90% of their holdings realized a trailing year return of - 19.3% as of August 2015. Investors who made practically no move returned - 3.7% over a similar period.

CHAPTER 15:
VARIOUS PRODUCT WE FIND INSIDE THE STOCK MARKET

Precious Metal

Silver and gold have been seen as noteworthy metals, and have been pining for a long time. In fact, even today, valuable metals have their place in a keen investor's portfolio. But, which valuable metal is best for investment purposes? What's more, for what reason would they say they are so volatile?

There are many ways to become tied up with precious metals like gold, silver, and platinum, and a large group of valid justifications why you should yield to the treasure hunt. So in case you're simply beginning out in precious metals, read on to become familiar with how they work and how you can invest in them.

Gold

We'll begin with the grand-daddy of all: gold. Gold is one of a kind for its solidness (it doesn't rust or erode), flexibility, and it's capacity to direct both heat and electricity. It has some industrial applications in dentistry and electronics, yet we know it essentially as a base for jewelry and as a type of currency.

The value of gold is controlled by the market 24 hours every day, seven days per week. Gold trades prevalently as a component of feeling—its cost is less influenced by the laws of supply and demand. This is because the new mine stock is boundlessly exceeded by the sheer size of over the ground, stored gold. To lay it out, when hoarders want to sell, the value drops. At the point when they need to purchase, another supply is immediately absorbed and the gold costs are driven higher.

Several factors account for an increased desire to hoard the shiny yellow metal:

Fundamental financial concerns: When banks and cash are viewed as flimsy and furthermore political dependability is inquire able, gold has routinely been searched out as a protected store of significant worth.

Inflation: When real rates of return in the equity, bond, or brokers markets are antagonistic, individuals consistently flock to gold as a benefit that will keep up its Value.

War or political emergencies: War and political change have constantly sent individuals into a gold-hoarding mode. A whole lifetime of Value of savings can be made portable and invest until it needs to be traded for foodstuffs, shelter or safe entry to a less dangerous destination.1 2

Silver

Unlike gold, the cost of silver swings between its apparent role as a store of significant Value and its role as an industrial metal. Thus, value fluctuations in the silver market are more volatile than gold.3 4

In this way, while silver will trade generally following gold as a thing to be stored (investment demand), the industrial supply/demand equation for the metal exerts a similarly solid impact on its cost. That condition has reliably fluctuated with developments, including:

Silver's once predominant role in the photography business—silver-based photographic film—which has been overshadowed by the appearance of the digital camera. The rise of a tremendous white-collar class in the developing market economies of the East, which made an unstable interest in electrical apparatuses, medical products, and other industrial items that require silver inputs. From direction to electrical associations, silver's properties made it a perfect item.

Silver's utilization in batteries, superconductor applications, and microcircuit markets. It's unclear whether, or to what degree, these improvements will influence overall non-investments demand for silver. One fact remains: Silver's cost is influenced by its applications and isn't simply utilized in fashion or as a store of value.5

Platinum

Like gold and silver, platinum is traded around the clock on global commodities markets. It will in general bring a more significant expense than gold during routine times of market and political stability simply because it's a lot rarer. Far less of the metal is pulled starting from the earliest stage.

There are likewise different variables that decide platinum's cost:

Like silver, platinum is seen as a modern metal. The best interest for platinum starts from car catalysts, which are used to lessen the hurtfulness of emanations. After this, gems accounts most of interest. Oil and synthetic refining forces and the PC enterprises go through the rest.

As a result of the auto industry's heavy reliance on the metal, platinum costs are resolved in enormous part via auto sales and production numbers. "Clean air" legislation could expect automakers to introduce more catalytic converters, raising demand. But, in 2009, American and Japanese vehicle creators began going to reused auto catalysts or utilizing a greater amount of platinum's dependable—and typically more affordable—sister group metal, palladium.6

Platinum mines are heavily concentrated in just two nations— South Africa and Russia.7 This makes more greater potential for cartel-like activity that would bolster or even misleadingly raise platinum costs.

Investors should consider that these components serve to make platinum the most unusual of the valuable metals.

Lesser known than the more than 3 is Palladium, which has progressively modern employments. Palladium is a gleaming, brilliant metal utilized in many kinds of manufacturing, especially for electronics and modern items. It can likewise be utilized in dentistry, medication, chemical applications, jewelry, and groundwater treatment. The vast majority of the world's supply of this uncommon metal, which has the atomic number 46 on the intermittent table of components, starts from mines arranged in the United States, Russia, South Africa, and Canada. Jewelers initially combined palladium into gems in 1939. Right when blended in with yellow gold, the amalgam shapes a metal more grounded than white gold. In 1967, the government of Tonga gave flowing palladium coins touting the crowning ordinance of King Taufa Ahau Tupou IV. This is the primary accounted case of palladium utilized in coinage.

Metalworkers can make slight sheets of palladium down to one-200 fifty thousandth of an inch. Pure palladium is pliable, yet it becomes more stronger and harder once someone works with the metal at room temperature. The sheets are then utilized in applications like solar energy and fuel cells.

The largest industrial use for palladium is in exhaust systems because the metal fills in as an incredible impetus that speeds up substance responses. This gleaming metal is 12.6% harder than platinum, making the element also more tough than platinum.

Filling Up Your Treasure Chest

We should investigate the options available to the individuals who need to invest in precious metals.

Commodity: Trade-traded brokers exist for every one of the three precious metals. ETFs are a helpful and liquid means for buying and selling gold, silver, or platinum. Investing in ETFs, however, doesn't give you access to the physical commodity, so you don't have a case on the metal in the fund. You won't get the genuine conveyance of a gold bar or silver coin.

Basic stocks and mutual fund: Shares of precious metals diggers are utilized to value developments in the precious metals. Except if you're mindful of how mining stocks are valued, it might be wiser to stick to brokers with managers with strong performance accounts.

Futures and choices: The possibilities and choices markets offer liquidity and impact to investors who need to make enormous bets on metals. The best potential benefits and misfortunes can be had with auxiliary things.

Bullion: Coins and bars are carefully for the individuals who have a place to put them like a safety deposit box or safe. Positively, for the individuals who are expecting the worst, bullion is the main alternative, yet for investors with a time skyline, bullion is illiquid and out and out vexatious to hold.

Certificates: Certificates offer investors all the advantages of physical gold possession without the issue of transportation and capacity. All things considered, in case you're searching for insurance in a real disaster, certificates are simply paper. Try not to anticipate that anybody should take them in return for anything of significant value.

Will Precious Metals Shine for You?

Valuable metals offer exceptional inflationary confirmation— they have trademark Value, they pass on no credit hazard, and they can't be expanded. That suggests you can't print a more prominent measure of them. They likewise offer real " upheaval insurance " against financial or political/military upheavals.

From an investment hypothesis outlook, precious metals likewise give low or negative connection to other resource classes like stocks and bonds. This suggests even somewhat level of valuable metals in a portfolio will diminish both unpredictability and hazard.

Valuable Metals Risks

Each investment accompanies its arrangement of risks. Although they may accompany a specific level of bonds, there is in every case some risk that accompanies investing in precious metals. Costs for metals can drop during times of economic sureness, putting a damper for people who like to put strongly in the valuable metals market. Selling may be a test during times of monetary unpredictability, as costs will when all is said in done shoot up. Finding a buyer for physical metals may be troublesome.

Another hazard to valuable metals costs fuses the issue of flexibly. Exactly when solicitation shoots up, the present flexibly may start to drain. What's more, that implies producers should bring a greater amount of each metal into the market. If there is a short supply of mineable metals, that could pressure on prices

Bonds

A bond is a kind of debt instrument gave and sold by a government, local authority, or organization to fund-raise. Investors who purchase bonds are paid interest, which for bonds is known as a "coupon".

The substance gets the brokers for a predetermined amount of time over which interest must be paid. At development, there is a last interest payment and return of head. The loan fee is dictated by the size of the coupon and the price of the bond at buy. If the bond is held to development, it additionally speaks to the rate of profit for the investments.

Bonds are ordinarily given at standard estimations of $100 or $1,000. Its real market cost will be subject to a mix of its term or time until maturity, credit quality, coupon rate, and the future anticipated direction of interest rates

The obtained brokers are regularly utilized for capital investment projects and to fund operations as well as financial activities, for example, inventory needs or to refinance current debt. Bond purchasers are regularly alluded to as debt holders or creditors.

Generally corporate and government bonds are traded on open trades. A few, be that as it may, are traded on over-the-counter markets, where purchasers and vendors trade securities without administrative oversight from a trade.

Kinds of Bonds

Fixed-rate bonds – The most widely recognized kind of bond, with a coupon that remaining parts fixed for the duration of the life of the bond. Bond coupons can likewise escalate in value throughout the life of the bond. This expands its term, given it pushes a greater amount of the income to be paid out sometime in the not too distant future, and builds its financing cost chance.

Zero-coupon bonds – Pays no interest, yet generally at a discount to par value (the degree of such relies upon an also evaluated coupon bond), with price appreciation basic leading the way to expiration. The principal cost is paid at maturity. Zero-coupon bonds, both fixed-rate and inflation ensured, are given by the US government. These are consistently called "strips", as the coupons are stripped out and can be exchanged independently from the bond itself. Given the higher span of these bonds, they are more insecure than standard coupon bonds.

Floating rate or inflation-indexed bonds – Bonds attached to some reference rate, for example, a particular LIBOR rate plus a spread, or attached to a measure of domestic inflation. Inflation and interest are unpredictability are two basic risks related to fixed-rate bonds. To represent this, a few contributions will give assurance against these risks by offering floating (or variable) rate bonds. Coupon rates are ordinarily recalculated each 1 a year. The UK was the principal government to give inflation filed bonds during the 1980s. The US gave its inflation ensured securities ("TIPS") starting in 1997.

High-yield bonds – Also known as "junk bonds". This differentiation incorporates bonds with a credit score beneath BBB-on the S&P and Fitch scale and Baa3 on the Moody's scale. The credit nature of these bonds is lower because of more elevated levels of financial risk that raises the backer's danger of bankruptcy. Investors hope to be made up for taking on higher risk. In this manner these bonds are viewed as "high return" comparative with an investment-grade bond.

Municipal bonds – Bonds gave by a city, state, province, or other local government. People are frequently boosted to invest in civil bonds through their tax-free structures. (In any case, this isn't in every case valid and relies upon the jurisdiction.)

Convertible bonds – Under specific conditions, a debt holder can change a bond to a specific number of shares of the issuer's basic stock. Since they consolidate debt and value qualities, they are viewed as crossbreed securities.

Indexed bonds – Bonds connected to a specific business indicator (i.e., net gain) or macroeconomic measurement (e.g., GDP). This structure is picked for organizations that need to have more power over their income by coordinating business execution with the payout of its bonds. Some civil bonds, known as income bonds, are filed to the revenue generated from the investment the bond continues funded.

Resource upheld securities (ABS) – Fixed-pay instruments where interest and principal payments are made sure about by the incomes of different assets. These can mortgage-backed securities (MBS), collateralized debt commitments (CDOs), understudy loans, charge card receivables, plane leases, among different assets. The individual segments to ABS are illiquid and by and large infeasible to sell separately, thus the need for securitization.

Investors take a look at ABS as an elective wellspring of fixed-salary investment and expansion. Assets are pooled and no single resource is commonly liable for outsized affecting its valuation. Guarantors frequently lean toward the ABS structure because the procedure of securitization permits them to move the fundamental assets off their asset reports and move the going with risk to a counterparty (the investors).

Covered bonds – Bonds supported public or private assets, for example, mortgages. Secured bonds contrast from ABS in that the assets remain on the issuer's balance sheet.

Climate or green bonds – Bonds gave by governments or enterprises to raise assets for environmental change alleviations or environmental preservation initiatives.

Mezzanine debt– Bonds, loan debt, or favored stock that speaks to a case on the organization's assets, just senior to that of basic offers. On account of a bankruptcy situation, loan bosses to the organization are repaid dependent on their chain of command in the capital structure.

Holders of senior debt made sure about by a case to assets of the organization will be preferred choice, trailed by junior/subjected debt holders, followed by preferred stockholders, lastly those holding normal stock. As a result of this payout progression, senior debt will have lower returns desires comparative with capital subjected to it, with basic offers having the most significant yields desires, holding all else equivalent.

On account of ABS, where various assets are packaged and pooled into a single bond, in case of default of certain securities, the ABS itself should in any case hold value, with senior tranches repaid before subjected tranches.

Perpetual bonds – Bonds with no development date. Known as perpetuities. These bonds issue coupon payments at regular intervals (ordinarily every 6 or a year) and will do as such into perpetuity. A few bonds that develop 100+ years later may likewise be labeled "perpetual" given their drawn-out nature.

Governments bonds – Bonds issued by a central government in created markets are regularly named "risk-free" given they are sponsored by the credit of the government. Given the typically strong credit height of these bonds, interest is commonly most minimal on these comparative with other fixed pay instruments. Also, given government agencies in developed economies run on fiat currency systems (i.e., not supported by an item by and large considered of significant value, and has value by government decree), it is constantly expected that government can pay their debt in nominal terms to avoid default if necessary, however conceivably to the expense of inflation.

Callable bonds – Bonds that the issuer can get back to from debt holders if loan costs tumble to some specified degree. This is done under the reason that less expensive financing can be gotten in place of the more costly bonds presently available. This gives guarantors more prominent power over financing costs. In any case, investors will generally demand extra remuneration for these due to the risk identified with these bonds being called.

Potable bonds – Bonds that can be returned to the issuer if loan cost rises fairly. This limits points financing cost risk on benefit of the interest of the investors. For the issuer, since they accept more interest rate risk, putable bonds are commonly a less expensive source of financing.

Precious stone

Gemstones are components of minerals which when cleaned and cut are utilized for making jewelry and different ornaments, just as for decoration purposes. Certain rocks or organic materials that are not considered as minerals are additionally expended in making jewelry products and are subsequently considered to gemstones too. While the vast majority of the gemstones are hard, certain delicate minerals are utilized in making gems inferable from their shine and different properties displaying stylish Value. Notwithstanding jewelry, hardstone carvings and relic diamonds have been significant extravagance works of art also. They are normally treated to improve the clarity or color of the stone, and can influence the estimation of the stone depending on the degree and sort of treatment. Certain gemstones are created to emulate different gemstones. Such gemstones incorporate manufactured moissanite and cubic zirconia which is a synthetic diamond stimulant comprising of zirconium oxide. These gemstones repeat the color and look the first stone yet don't display their physical and chemical properties. Moissanite has a higher refractive index as compared to diamond and has more "fire" when given a comparable cut and estimated diamond. The worldwide interest for gemstones has been noteworthy owing to consumers opting for buying medium estimated gem items utilizing specific stages, for example, home shopping through TV advertising. While the mid-extending shoppers lean toward buying limited items, top buyers are picking towards investing in jewelry and gems. Also, certain elements, for example, fashion designers centering towards creating innovative gems items just as producers turning out to be vertically incorporated engaged with creating gemstones just as jewelry are contributing towards the growth of the gemstones market.

Gemstones share a wide application scope in making jewelry. The market for jewelry and gems has been seeing a significant increase in extra cash of the people combined with developing utilization of ornaments in ceremonies in Asian economies. Consumers in developing economies, for example, Asia Pacific are gradually drifting away from the customary unorganized jewelry and slanting towards composed branded products to shield themselves from counterfeit. Besides, rising mindfulness concerning the advantages of shopping from composed retail by actualizing different limited time techniques and commercials has additionally prompted expanding utilization of jewelry which has additionally contributed towards the demand for gemstones in the Asia Pacific and different regions. Expanding interest for jewelry just as the incorporation of gems in jewelry items attributable to expanding spending of the consumers just as changing the way of life is required to drive the demand for jewelry items over the figure time frame along these lines expanding the demand for gemstones. Likewise, expanding the utilization of diamonds as an individual element for design reasons for existing is additionally expected to invest in the developing utilization of gemstones. Be that as it may, factors, for example, rising labor charges just as inflation affecting the costs of jewelry are along these lines expected to adversely influence the development of its raw materials, for example, gemstones. Concentrate on innovative work exercises towards creating innovative items just as a spotlight on showcase extension in the emerging region, for example, Latin America and Asia Pacific are relied upon to give new chances to the growth of the market.

Forex

Forex is a portmanteau of remote cash and exchange. Outside exchange is the route toward transforming one cash into another money for an assortment of reasons, generally speaking for business, exchanging, or the travel industry. As showed by an ongoing triennial report from the Bank for

International Settlements (an overall bank for national banks), the ordinary was more than $5.1 trillion in step by step forex exchanging volume.1

What Is the Forex Market?

The outside exchange advertise is the spot monetary standards are exchanged. Monetary forms are essential to a great many people the world over, regardless of whether they understand it or not, on the grounds that monetary standards principles ought to be exchanged to coordinate outside exchange and business. In the event that you are living in the U.S. besides, need to buy cheddar from France, it is conceivable that you or the organization that you buy the cheddar from requirements to pay the French for the cheddar in euros (EUR). This suggests the U.S. importer would need to exchange the equivalent estimation of U.S. dollars (USD) into euros. The proportionate goes for voyaging. A French tourist in Egypt can't pay in euros to see the pyramids since it's not the secretly acknowledged money. In that capacity, the tourist needs to trade the euros for the local currency, for this situation the Egyptian pound, at the current trade rate.

One exceptional part of this global market is that there is no central marketplace for foreign trade. Or maybe, currency trading is conducted electronically over-the-counter (OTC), which implies that all trades happen to employ computer networks between traders around the world, instead of on one centralized trade. The market is open 24 hours out of each day, five and a half days seven days, and monetary standards are exchanged worldwide the significant cash money related focuses of London, New York, Tokyo, Zurich, Frankfurt, Hong Kong, Singapore, Paris and Sydney—across basically every time zone. This implies when the trading day the U.S. ends, the forex market starts once more in Tokyo and Hong Kong. Accordingly, the forex market can be incredibly dynamic whenever of the day, with value cites evolving continually.

Currency as an Asset Class

There are two particular highlights to currencies as an asset class:

- You can gain the interest fee differential between two currencies.
- You can benefit from changes in the trade rate.

An investor can benefit from the difference between two loan costs in two unique economies by purchasing the currency with the higher interest rate and shorting the cash with a lower interest rate. Preceding the 2008 financial crisis, it was exceptionally normal to short the Japanese yen (JPY) and buy British pounds (GBP) because the interest rate differential was very large. This technique is once in a while alluded to as a "carry trade."

Why We Can Trade Currencies

Currency trading was exceptionally hard for singular investors preceding the internet. Most currency traders were multinational organizations, hedge investments, or high-net Value people because forex trading required a ton of capital. With assistance from the internet, a retail showcase focused on individual traders has risen, giving simple access to the outside foreign trade markets, either through the banks themselves or intermediaries making a secondary market. Most online brokers or dealers offer high impact to traders who can control an enormous exchange with a little record balance.

Forex Trading Risks

Exchanging monetary forms can be perilous and complex. The interbank market has differing degrees of guideline, and forex instruments are not standardized. In specific bits of the world, forex exchanging is unregulated.

The interbank showcase is involved banks exchanging with each other around the world. The banks themselves need to choose and recognize credit risk and sovereign risk, and they have set up inside strategies to secure themselves as could sensibly be normal. Rules like this are industry-constrained for the affirmation of each partaking bank.

Since the market is made by every one of the partaking banks giving offers and offers to a specific currency, the market pricing mechanism is based on supply and demand. Since there are such large trade flows inside the system, it is hard for rogue traders to impact the cost of a currency. This system makes transparency in the market for investors with access to interbank dealing.

Retail traders' trade with respectably semi-unregulated and little forex agents/dealers, which can (and some of the time do) re-provide cost estimates and even exchange against their clients. Depending on where the dealer exists, there might be some government and industry regulation, however, those safeguards are conflicting far and wide.

Most retail investors ought to spend time investigating a forex dealer to see if it is directed in the U.S. or then again the U.K. (dealers in the U.S. also, U.K. have more oversight) or in a country with lax rules and oversight. It is likewise a smart thought to discover what kind of account securities are accessible in a market emergency, or if a dealer becomes insolvent.

CHAPTER 16:
SECTORS WHERE IT IS WORTH INVESTING

Best Sectors to Beat the Market in the Long Term

If you need to beat the stock market averages over some time, one approach to do it is to invest in the best divisions that have the best potential for growing faster than the general economy over the long term. What's more, an incredible method to get focused exposure to these sectors is with sector brokers.

Diversified mutual fund - those that don't concentrate on one sector - will as of now have presentation to most industry areas. For instance, an S&P 500 Index fund gives exposure to sectors, for example, health care, energy, technology, utilities, and financial companies. However, if you need to beat the S&P 500, the most ideal approach to do it is by assigning more of your portfolio assets to the sectors that can be the leaders of tomorrow.

Step by step instructions to choose the Best Sector Brokers as long as possible

Choosing the best sectors to purchase for the future doesn't take mind-blowing luck or a lot of research. Everything necessary is a brief investigation of trends and a bit of common sense.

Here are the absolute best sorts of part assets to purchase for what's to come:

Technology Sector Brokers: Technology is at the edge of innovation and at the central point of the Information Age, which makes certain to proceed for a considerable length of time. The technology sector is a class of stocks that contains technological organizations, for instance, makers creating PC hardware, PC soft or gadgets and technological service industry associations, for instance, those giving information technology and business data processing. A few instances of technology organizations incorporate Apple (AAPL), Microsoft (MSFT), Google (GOOG) and Facebook (FB). What's more, other tech organizations make certain to join innovations we are not thinking about today.

Health Care Sector Brokers: With an aging population and rapid advances in biotechnology, the health industry is certain to flourish in the years and decades ahead. The healthcare sector is very wide. Indeed, even an individual with no investing experience can think about some particular zone of the health industry, for example, hospital conglomerates, institutional services, insurance agencies, drug manufacturers, biomedical companies, or medical instrument producers. Likewise, when many industries are doing poorly due to negative economic conditions, the health industry can even now perform relatively well since individuals despite everything need to see the doctor and buy their medications, paying little mind to economic conditions. Hence the healthcare sector is considered as a "defensive sector."

Financials Sector Brokers: The financial related services sector (aka "financials") comprises principally of banks, credit card companies, insurance companies, and brokerage firms. Similar to the health sector, financials stand to benefit from the time of increased birth rates age, who are relied upon to get the biggest trade of riches in history as their parents die pass along their life savings to them. Financial firms that can benefit include banks, brokerage firms, and insurance companies.

Diversified Investment

Diversified investment is an arrangement of different resources that wins the best yield for the least risk. A diversified portfolio has a blend of stocks, fixed compensation, and things. Diversification works because the advantages respond diversely to the equivalent economic occasion.

In a diversified portfolio, the assets don't connect. At the point when the estimation of one rises, the value of different falls. It brings down overall risk because, regardless of what the economy does, some asset classes will profit. That offsets losses in other assets. Risk is additionally in light of the fact that it's uncommon that the entire portfolio would be cleared out by any single occasion. A broadened portfolio is your best defend against a money related crisis.1

Case of How Diversification Works

Stocks do well when the economy develops. Financial specialists need the most significant yields, so they offer up the expense of stocks. They are happy to recognize a more serious danger of a downturn since they are idealistic about what's to come. Investors are keen on ensuring their property in a downturn. They are willing to acknowledge lower returns for that reduction of risk.

The costs of items change with supply and demand. Commodities include wheat, oil, and gold. For instance, wheat costs would rise if there is a dry spell that limits supply. Oil costs would fall if there is extra flexibly. Therefore commodities don't follow the periods of the business cycle as intently as stocks and bonds.

Include These Six Asset Classes to Diversify Your Portfolio

A diversified portfolio ought to contain securities from the following six asset classes:

- U.S. stocks. Diverse measured companies ought to be included. Company size is estimated by its market capitalization. In this way, incorporate small-cap, mid-top, and large-cap in any portfolio.
- U.S. fixed salary. The safest are U.S. Treasury and saving bonds. These are ensured by the federal government. Municipal bonds are likewise very safe. You can likewise purchase bond brokers and brokerage brokers that invest in these safe securities. Corporate bonds furnish a better return with more prominent risk. The most significant yields and risks accompany garbage bonds.
- Foreign stocks. These incorporate organizations from both created and developing markets. You can accomplish more greater diversification if you invest abroad. Worldwide investments can produce a better yield because developing markets nations are becoming quicker. Yet, they are more dangerous investments because these nations have less national bank shields set up, can be vulnerable to political changes, and are less transparent.
- Foreign investments likewise fence against a declining dollar. U.S. organizations do well when the dollar is feeble because it supports trades. Foreign organizations do well when the dollar is solid. That makes their

exports into the United States less cheaper than when the dollar is weak.

- Foreign fixed income. These incorporate both corporate and government issues. They give assurance from a dollar decline. They are more secure than foreign stocks.
- Commodities. This incorporates natural resources, for example, gold, oil, and land. Gold ought to be a piece of any diversified investment since it's the best fence against a stock market crash. Research shows that gold costs rise drastically for 15 days after the crash. This is the reason individuals invest in gold. Gold can be a decent defense against inflation. It is additionally uncorrelated to assets, for example, stocks and bonds.

You ought to remember the value of your home in your diversification strategy.

A type of commodity that should be considered a sixth asset class is the equity in your home. Most investment advisors don't include the value in your home as a real investment. They assume you will keep on living there for the rest of your life. At the end of the day, they believe it to be a consumable item, similar to a vehicle or a refrigerator, not an investment.

That urged many homeowners to borrow against the value in their homes to buy other buyer products. When housing prices declined, they owed more than the house was Value. Accordingly, many individuals lost their homes during the financial emergency. Some left their homes while others declared bankruptcy

If your value goes up, you can sell other brokers investments, for example, REITs or brokers investment trusts, in your portfolio. You may likewise think about selling your home, taking a few benefits, and moving into a little house. This will keep you from being house-rich however cash poor. At the end of the day, you won't have all your investment eggs in your home basket.

Diversification and Asset Allocation

What amount would it be a good idea for you to claim asset class? There is nobody size-fits-all best-diversified investment.

Investors use asset allocation to decide the specific blend of stocks, bonds, and products. It relies upon your comfort with various risk levels, your objectives, and where you are in life. For instance, stocks are less secure than bonds. If you need the cash in the next few years, you should hold more bonds than somebody who could hold up 10 years. Along these lines, the level of each sort of asset class relies upon your objectives. They ought to be created with a financial planner.

You ought to likewise rebalance depending upon the current period of the business cycle. In the beginning period of a recovery, small businesses do the best. They are the first to see opportunities and can react more quickly than large firm. Colossal top stocks do well in the last piece of a recovery. They have more agents to advertise the littler organizations.

Be careful with asset bubbles. That is the point at which the cost of any asset class rises quickly. It's being offered up by speculators. It isn't upheld by fundamental genuine values. Regular rebalancing will shield you from asset bubbles. You should sell any advantage that is developed so much it takes up a lot of your portfolio. If you follow this discipline, you won't get hit too hard when the bubble bursts.

In a well-diversified portfolio, the most important assets don't associate with other assets.[1] since the financial crisis, stocks and things have been identified with a connected of 0.6. So have U.S. stocks and made worldwide markets at 0.93. If you have U.S. stocks, there are no broadening advantages to having created markets in your portfolio. They move a similar way stocks do.

At the point when a Mutual Fund Is a Diversified Investment

A mutual fund or index fund gives more diversification than individual bonds. They track a stack of stocks, bonds, or products. A common or index fund would be an enhanced investment if it contained every one of the six asset classes. To address your needs, it would likewise need to adjust those assets according to your objectives. At that point, it would adjust depending upon the phase of the business cycle.

Common Investing Mistakes You Need to Avoid

No one's perfect. We are all going to have our successes and losses. However, some of the slip-ups you may make when trading stocks are in reality quite normal, and in no way, reserved exclusively for only you — most of the investors commit a large number of the following errors.

Truth be told, at times, the investor may keep on committing the same error many occasions over, when they don't learn from their past errors. Maybe you have some immediate experience with just precisely such a circumstance.

Fortunately the greater part of these mistakes can be dodged just through awareness. We will take a look at the most widely recognized mistakes here, and identify ways by which might have the option to stop the bleeding (or even make them advantageous for you).

Purchasing Shares in a Business Which You Do Not Understand

Time after time investors float towards the most recent "hot" or extravagant sounding industry. They may know practically nothing, about technology, or biotech, or the particular business the underlying organization is locked in inside.

That doesn't prevent them from attempting to bounce on to what they hope to be the following beneficial train. In this situation, the investor is disregarding all the advantages and benefits they would have over investors who think little about the industry itself.

At the point when you understand a business, you have a normally worked in advantage over most other investors. For instance, if you run a restaurant you'll be in line with organizations associated with restaurant franchising.

You will likewise observe direct (and before they become public knowledge) the habits for the supporters. By expansion you will know whether the industry is booming, getting slower, or chilling off, a long time before by far most of investors.

To make our situation a step further, by observing the trends in the industry in which you are locked in, you ought to have the option to spot a few opportunities to settle on incredible investments choices. First-hand knowledge, doubtlessly, can mean investment profits (or avoiding losses).

At the point when you invest in an organization that is "over your pay grade," you may not comprehend the subtleties and the complexity of the business being referred to. It is not necessarily the case that you should be a gold miner to invest in gold mining organizations, or a medical doctor to invest in healthcare, however that surely wouldn't do any harm!

Whenever you can have an out of line advantage over most investors, you should press that advantage as far as a lawyer; you may improve realizing when to invest in organizations that make their incomes through litigation. If that you are a medical surgeon, you'll have a prevalent understanding of how well (or inadequately) a medical procedure robot is playing out their task, and as such may have an inside track on how well the principal stock may perform.

Anticipating Too Much From the Stock

This is especially evident when managing penny stocks. A lot of people treat low-cost stocks like lottery tickets, and envision that they can change their $500 or $2000 into a small fortune.

This can in some cases be valid, yet it's anything but a suitable mentality to have when you're getting into investing. You should be practical about what you will anticipate from the performance of the shares, regardless of whether such numbers are substantially more boring and mundane than the pure fantasy levels for which you may hope.

Take a look at the performance of the stock up until this point. Additionally, observe the various investments that are rivals in a similar industry. Truly, has the basic investments picked up 5% or 10% every year, or have those draws been nearer to several rates? Do most organizations in the business see their shares moving 1% at once, or is it progressively regular for them to hop by many rates?

In light of the past exhibition, while not demonstrative of what might be to come, you could get a thought of the unpredictability and trading movement of the hidden offers. Commonly, a stock will keep on acting primarily as it has previously, and for the most part that will be in line with the general industry.

Utilizing Money You Cannot Afford to Risk

You would be overwhelmed if you could perceive how extraordinary your trading style becomes when you are utilizing cash which you can't bear to risk. Your feelings get increased, your anxiety experiences the rooftop, and you settle on purchase and sell choices which you in any case would have never made.

An old Japanese proverb says that, "you will, in the long run, lose each dollar with which you bet." You should never place yourself into the high-pressure circumstance where you are risking cash which you need for different reasons.

The first idea is to just to invest in quite a while with 'risk money.' However, we can make it a step further, and propose that you don't utilize genuine cash when you are beginning. Consider Paper Trading, which is no-risk, and requires no cash at all. At that point, when you get good at Paper Trading, you can migrate towards trading real money.

At the point when you invest with money that you can afford to risk, you will make more relaxed trading decisions, For the most part, you will have substantially more accomplishment with your trades, which won't be driven by negative emotions or fear.

Being Driven by Impatience

We may have touched on the various feelings you can have when you're investing, yet one of the most costly ones is restlessness. Recollect that stocks are shares in a particular business — businesses operate considerably more gradually than the vast majority of us might commonly want to see, or even than most of us would anticipate.

At the point when the management thinks of another strategy, it might take many months, if not quite a long while, for that new way to deal with begin playing out. Too often investors will buy shares of the stock, and afterward promptly anticipate that the shares to act in their best interest.

This ignores the significantly more reasonable timeline under which organizations work. All in all, stocks will take any longer to make the moves that you are seeking after or anticipating. At the point when individuals initially engage with shares of the organization, they should not let restlessness get the best of them... or their wallet!

Finding out About Stocks to Invest in From the Wrong Places

This is a critical point. There is no deficiency of purported experts who are eager to disclose to you their sentiments, while packaging and introducing them as though they are educated and endlessly correct knowledge.

One of the most critical parts to investing admirably is to recognize and confine sources of direction which reliably assist you with accomplishing benefits. For each great piece of information that might be of advantage, you will most likely observe several bits of extremely awful direction.

Always remember that since somebody is being included or met by top media, doesn't mean they recognize what they are discussing. Furthermore, regardless of whether they do have a stellar grasp of their topic, which despite everything doesn't mean they will be correct.

Along these lines, your activity as an investor is to evaluate which sources of information ought to be trusted, and have exhibited a dependable and continuous pattern of wisdom. When you have distinguished those people or administration which may prompt benefits, you should in any case just somewhat depend on their thoughts — join those with your due diligence and opinions to build trading choices.

If you catch wind of a stock for nothing, particularly a penny stock, it is more likely than not being driven by players with noteworthy concealed inspirations. This may not be true if you hear about an expert's opinion on something, for example, CNBC, however, it is completely and un-completely obvious when you find out about the most recent "hot penny stock" that will experience the rooftop (as indicated by greedy advertisers).

There is an interminable line of deceptive stock advertisers out there. Their fixation is to discover approaches to benefit from your activities... you lose, so they can pick up.

The awful side is that for them to benefit, you will most likely need to lose. Investing in speculative shares is for the most part a zero-sum game, which means for somebody to make a dollar, another person needs to lose a dollar.

This is the reason scam artists and advertisers take such endeavors to drive up useless offers. The more cash they get the opportunity to push the stock costs higher, the more prominent the benefit they'll make when they leave and leave every other person in the dust... and broke.

Following the Crowd

By and large, most of individuals possibly find out about an investment when it has already performed well. If particular sorts of stocks twofold or triple in value, the predominant media will in general spread that move, and inform everybody regarding how hot the shares have been.

Sadly, when the media will in general engage with an anecdote about shares rising, it is typically after the stock has arrived at its peak. The investment is exaggerated by this point, and the media inclusion arrives behind schedule to the game. In any case, the TV, paper, web, and radio coverage push the stocks significantly higher into unnecessarily exaggerated territory.

We have seen this pattern play out as of late with the recreational weed stocks. Some of these small organizations had just a few employees, however, that didn't prevent them from being valued at a corporate Value of about half of one billion dollars!

On different occasions, an old almost old gold mine would include 'cannabis' or 'pot' to the name of their organization, and the offers would in a split second twofold or triple in cost. At no time were investors investigating the organization sufficiently deep to understand all the issues; a huge number of dollars owing debtors; no incomes; millions in continuous losses every month.

Averaging Down

Averaging down is normally utilized by investors who have committed an error as of now, and they have to cover over their mistake. For instance, if they purchased the stock at $3.50, and it drops to $1.75, they can commit that error look somewhat less awful by buying an entire pack more offers at this new, lower cost.

The outcome is that presently they've purchased stock at $3.50, and more at $1.75, so their normal cost per share is a lot of lower. This causes their loss on the stock to show up far smaller.

However, it is truly happening that the individual purchased a stock which dropped in Value, and now they are sinking much more cash into this losing trade. This is the reason some analysts recommend that averaging down is simply wasting valuable assets.

Averaging down is commonly utilized as a support to assist investors with covering the mix-up they have just made. A progressively powerful strategy is to average up, where you buy to a greater degree a stock once it begins to move toward the path you are anticipating. The offer value action is affirming that you made a good call.

Doing Too Little Due Diligence

To do the best possible measure of due constancy, particularly with highly theoretical and unstable penny stock offers, it takes a lot of work. The more due determination you play out, the better your investing outcomes will turn into.

If you take a look at warning sign and each part of an organization, you're substantially less prone to be shocked by any individual occasion which afflicts the business. At the point when you see the potential risks, and you feel positive about all the parts of the organization into which you've been looking, you are part approach to having performed proper due diligence.

Most by far of investors don't verge on doing what's necessary due constancy into the organizations that they invest into. The vast majority simply need to discover an organization that appears to make sense, and should increment in value because the basic industry (in any event in their psyche) is "cutting-edge."

For instance, electric vehicles will turn into a greater deal soon, so individuals may expect that investing in an electric vehicle stock is a smart thought. Lamentably, to be a good investor takes significantly more than the rearranged, surface contemplations, and shallow logic.

If you think about the turn-of-the-century, there were more than 1,900 vehicle companies in America. The car would have been a major, significant invention that we could never be without... yet pretty much every one of these 1,900 companies went bankrupt.

The final product is that most investors in car companies at the earliest reference point, when the adoption and growth of this groundbreaking idea was simply getting started, injury up getting cleared out. Some improved due determination would have maintained a strategic distance from the losses.

Investing Based on a Single Concept

Most investors don't understand they're doing this, however, a great deal of times they will accept that 'such and such' is a smart thought, and consequently the stock cost will increase. If investing were that simple, we would all be exceptionally rich.

Indeed, a remedy for cancer is an extraordinary thought. Indeed, producing municipality incomes through deals of weed appears to be sensible. Tragically, it takes much more than a straightforward smart thought for the offers to be a wise investment.

CHAPTER 17:
ONLINE STOCK MARKET

A Few Advantages and Disadvantages of Online-Based Trading

With online trading, traders settle on the entirety of their choices themselves. Such an approach contrasts from utilizing a stockbroker, as the dealer commonly offers info and advice. Despite how you trade, there's consistently risk. Here are five favorable circumstances and weaknesses of online trading.

Online trading keeps on getting popularity. More than 14 million family units in the U.S. are joined with an online trading service, as indicated by data from Statistic, a measurement company.

With online trading, or e-trading, traders settle on the entirety of their choices themselves. Such a way to deal with trading differs from utilizing a stockbroker, as the representative commonly offers information and advice.

Despite of how you trade, there's reliably risk online and off. The going with list outlines the advantages and disadvantages of online trading.

5 advantages of internet trade

1. Lower charges

175

One of the most clearest points of online trade is the decrease in transaction cost and high charges identified with traditional brick and mortar business firms. Regularly, you'll pay somewhere in the range of $5 and $10 to purchase and sell stocks and trade brokers at online discount brokerages, as indicated by a Bloomberg report.

2. More control and adaptability

Time is normally of the quintessence when you trade stocks, so the speed of using online trade portals is an advantage to many investors. With online trade, you can execute a trade very quickly. Traditional physical agents may require arrangements, online, via telephone, or face to face, just to start a trade.

3. Capacity to stay away from business inclination

By taking trading into your own hands, you can wipe out brokerage bias. Inclination now and then happens when a broker offers financial guidance that benefits the broker —, for example, as a commission for selling explicit mutual funds and different items.

4. Access to online instruments

In the realm of online trading, a lower cost doesn't mean a disgraceful item. A significant number of the present online trading organizations offer clients a noteworthy suite of tools giving important information and helping optimize trades.

5. Option to monitor investments in real-time

Many online trading sites offer stock statements and trade information that make it simple for individuals to perceive how their investments are doing in real-time.

5 disadvantages of online trading

1. Easier to invest too much too fast

Since online trading is so easy — you fundamentally press a button — there is the risk of settling on poor investment decisions or overinvesting.

Online investors can secure themselves by understanding the stocks they are purchasing and setting up shields in quick rated markets. Submitting a breaking point request for you is one approach to control what you purchase and its amount.

2. No personal relationships with brokers

From finding support on the most proficient method to make an investment strategy to understanding how the results of criticism components influence the market, online traders are left to their own devices. For some, this kind of autonomy can be unsettling.

Experts often stress the significance of research, especially for new traders. You have to learn as much as possible about the companies in which you invest.

3. Addictive nature

Online traders can encounter a specific high when trading that is like what individuals experience when betting, as per an ongoing report on over the top trading distributed the diary Addictive Behaviors. The investigation noticed that a few investors choose short-term trading strategies that involve investing in risky stocks offering the potential for large gains yet additionally critical losses. "The structure itself of the two exercises (gambling and trading) is extremely close," the study finished up.

4. Internet-dependent

The nature of online trading implies that, at last, you're helpless before your internet connection. If the internet connection is too slow is interfered with, you can lose out on a conceivably significant or rewarding trade.

5. Buying errors due to computer missteps

With online trading, to just accept a trade was not finished can cost you cash. Investors who accept their trade was not finished may make the trade again and wind up investing twice as much as they planned. Accepting a trade was finished without seeing confirmation of the reality likewise is a mix-up. Ensure you see how to confirm trade and review statements before you start utilizing an online investing system.

Best Stock Trading Apps

In the course of the most recent couple of years, online brokers have progressively embraced the mantra, "mobile-first." As more investors and traders use tablets or cell phones as their essential stage, online intermediaries have put forth attempts to improve their versatile applications, which thusly draw in increasingly mobile users. The best online investing applications offer a steady encounter among work area and mobile platforms, including sharing watch accounts and cautions just as devices, for example, stock screeners and keeping looks into your account.

- TD Ameritrade: Best Stock Trading App
- TD Ameritrade: Best App for Beginners
- Intelligent Brokers: Best App for Active Traders

- Tastyworks: Best App for Options Traders

The Most Effective Method To Choose A Trading Site

1. Charges

One of the primary interesting points before picking which trading platform to invest your cash and time on charges. While trading can be a beneficial method to invest, commissions and expenses can truly eat into your benefits, so picking a reasonable platform is fundamental. There is noteValuey fluctuation between trading platform with regards to expenses, yet as a rule, you ought to know about the accompanying charges while choosing a stage

Account essentials

The primary cost you should confront when online trading is the minimum deposit. Trading platform frequently charges minimum deposits, which are not real expenses since it is cash that will be quickly accessible in your account once you store it, anyway it merits remembering particularly if your capital is constrained in which case you may need to raise brokers to start trading. The most reduced least store stage is Stash Invest, which requires $5 just to put your first trade, making it the best trading platform for investors who may have a constrained funding in any case. This is trailed by $50 at eToro (for US clients) and $100 at Plus500.

Trading expenses

Trading fees are the most widely recognized concerning online trading platforms. These incorporate commissions and spreads. Dealers may charge fixed spread, variable spread, or commission-based spreads. Significantly, you read about the platform's trading charges detail before you start trading as this can influence your main concern. A few intermediaries may likewise have concealed for the time being trading charges. eToro is an incredible decision for U.S. clients as they have one of the most reasonable, straightforward trading charges.

Non-trading Fees

Non-trading charges identify with trade expenses, withdrawal expenses, etc. The best decision if we consider non-trading expenses alone is Plus500. The platform charges genuinely high trading expenses, however it doesn't charge any non-trading charges. Underneath we clarify some regular non-trading charges:

Store charges

Deposit fees are applied when you send cash to your trading account from your bank account. Most platforms will in general offer free deposits, yet if you are keeping brokers with a universal bank card, you should look out for change rate charges.

Withdrawal charges

A few agents may charge an expense when you pull back your assets. eToro, for example, charges $5 expense on all withdrawals. The base withdrawal sum is $50.

Inactivity fees: Many trading platforms likewise charge a latency expense when you quit trading for a given timeframe. This implies you should be key about your trading action to abstain from getting charged after a more drawn out time of no trade. If you are a purchase and hold a financial specialist, you might need to avoid platforms with such charges.

Account fees: It isn't phenomenal for some trading platform to charge an account expense as level monthly payments, particularly with regards to share managing or stock trading platforms, for example, IG. None of the platforms in this book charge account expenses.

The least expensive stage in the agents we accounted for is Stash Invest, with charges beginning at $1 every month. In case you're UK based, attempt Plus500 who offers low spreads from 1.9 pips. Notwithstanding, remember that they do charge a latency expense of $10, and some short-term and interest expenses may apply.

2. Platform

Trading tools

The trading tools accessible rely upon the actual trading platform you are utilizing. We consider MetaTrader4 or MT5 to be the best trading platform out there. The main representative out of the ones we accounted for that utilizes MT4 is Libertex. Different stages utilize various kinds of trading spaces, although they are similarly proficient.

Speed and order execution

The execution speed is an indispensable component to consider particularly for a day investors. When trading or investing in quick-moving markets, the contrast among losing and increasing a large number of dollars can come down to a couple of milliseconds. In this manner, we recommend ensuring that the stage you pick can stay aware of your trading demands.

Copy-trading

Some trading platforms offer the copy trading choice, which permits brokers to put indistinguishable trades from proficient dealers. This specific component is the thing that makes eToro stand apart from the crowd. We believe it to be outstanding amongst other social trading agents, and a perfect decision if you are a learner and don't have a reasonable trading strategy in mind yet.

In case you're increasingly experienced, and are situated in the UK, Plus500 offers an incredible trading platform.

3. Asset Classes and Variety

Something else to consider while picking your online trading platforms are the sorts of benefits they offer and the variety. Resource variety and broadening are one of the most basic trading methodologies and can help take your trading to the following level by adjusting your portfolio and balancing risks.

One reason why Plus500 is among our most suggested trading platform for the UK is its advantage variety. You will have the option to pick between more than 2,000 instruments.

4. Regulation

Regulation is another significant factor to consider while picking an online trading website. At whatever point we audit trading platforms, one of the principal things we take a look at is whether they are managed by money related bodies.

Holding a permit implies that organizations monitor how the investment association's tasks intently. To keep up their administrative status, the organization needs to submit to rules intended to ensure the interests of customers.

The greater part of the platforms we suggest in this book are regulated. The best trading platform for guideline and bonds incorporate eToro for example (CySEC and FCA) and Plus500 (FCA guideline and accounted on the London Stock Trade)

5. Usability

Convenience has to do effortlessly of utilization of the trading platform general just as the sign-up and confirmation process. All things considered, if you are serious about investing, you may wind up investing a ton of energy in the platform, so you need to evade whatever number snags as could reasonably be expected. All the stages we suggest have genuinely straightforward sign-up forms and instinctive interfaces.

Something else to consider in online trading is that many individuals mistake multifaceted nature for viability. Most tenderfoots get overpowered when they discover a platform that offers many features. They imagine that an entangled platform means a viable one and overlook the idea of ease of use. Gaining admittance to various features won't make you an effective dealer.

A trading space that you find too confused may overpower you and keep you from making the most out of your trading experience. Ensure you acclimate yourself with the merchant's foundation before you begin investing in it. If you don't feel good with it, we propose proceeding onward to an alternate trading platform.

Brokers vs Bank: What's the Difference?

Dealers versus Market Producer: An Outline

Different players take part in the market. These incorporate purchasers, dealers, sellers, intermediaries, and market creators. Some help to encourage deals between two parties, while others help make liquidity or the accessibility to purchase and sell in the market. A dealer brings in cash by uniting advantages for buyers and sellers.

Then again, a market marker helps create an opportunity for investors to purchase or sell securities. In this book, we'll diagram the contrasts among brokers and market makers.

Broker

In the financial world, brokers are middle people who have the approval and aptitude to purchase securities on an investors' sake. The speculations that merchants offer consolidate protections, stocks, shared intermediaries, exchange exchanged resources (ETFs), and even real estate. Mutual funds and ETFs are comparative items in that the two of them contain a bushel of securities, for example, stocks and bonds.

Brokers are controlled and authorized. Brokers must enrol with the Financial Industry Regulatory Authority (FINRA) while investment guides register through the U.S. Protections and Exchange Commission (SEC) as Registered Investment

Advisors or RIAs. Agents resolve to act to the best preferred position of their clients.

Many brokers can likewise offer advice on which stocks, mutual funds, and different securities to purchase. Also, with the accessibility of online trading platforms, many investors can start trades with practically zero contact with their merchants. Although there are different kinds of dealers, they can be separated into two classifications.

Full-Service Brokers

Full-administration brokers give their customers more Value included services. These administrations may incorporate counseling, research, investment advice, and retirement arranging. Many intermediaries give trading platforms, trade execution benefits, and altered theoretical and supporting arrangements with the utilization of alternatives contracts. Choices contracts are subsidiaries meaning they get their incentive from a basic resource. Choices give investors the right, however not the commitment to purchase or sell securities at a preset cost where the agreement terminates later on.

For these administrations, investors generally pay higher commissions for their trades. Brokers likewise get pay dependent on the number of new accounts they acquire and their customers' trading volume. Brokers charge expenses for investment items just as oversaw investment accounts. A few dealers take into account high-total assets customers with assets of $1 at least a million.

Discount Brokers

With advancements in technology and the internet, online business firms have encountered a blast of development. These rebate intermediaries permit investors to trade at a lower cost, however, there's a catch; investors don't get the customized investment advice that is offered by full-administration brokers.

The diminished commission can go from around $5 to $15 per trade. The low expenses depend on trading volume, and since there's no investment advice, representatives of online brokers are normally repaid by compensation rather than commission. Many discount brokers offer online trading platforms, which are perfect for self-coordinated traders and investors.

Market Maker

Banks are regularly huge banks or money related institutions. They help to guarantee there's sufficient liquidity in the markets, which means there's a sufficient volume of trading so traders should be possible consistently. Without market makers, there would almost certainly be little liquidity. At the end of the day, investors who need to sell securities would be not able to loosen up their situations because of an absence of buyers in the market.

Banks help keep the market working, which means if you need to sell a bond, they are there to get it. So also, if you need to purchase a stock, they're there to have that stock accessible to offer to you.

Banks are helpful because they are constantly prepared to purchase and sell as long as the investor is happy to address a particular cost. Banks go about as wholesalers by purchasing and offering securities to fulfill the market—the costs they set reflect showcase the organic market. At the point when the interest for bonds is low, and supply is high, the cost of the bonds will below. If the interest is high and supply is low, the cost of the bonds will be high. Banks are committed to sell and purchase at the cost and size they have cited.

Some of the time a market maker is likewise a broker, which can make a motivation for a broker to suggest securities for which the firm additionally makes a market. Investors should along these lines perform due tirelessness to ensure that there is an unmistakable partition between a broker and a market maker.

A few instances of the greater Banks in the business incorporate BNP Paribas, Deutsche Bank, Morgan Stanley, and UBS.

How Banks Make Money

Banks charge a spread on the purchase and sell cost, and execute on the two sides of the market. Market maker set up cites for the bid and asks costs, or purchase and sell costs. Investors who need to sell bonds would get the offer value, which would be somewhat lower than the real cost. If investors needed to purchase bonds, they would get charged the ask value, which is set somewhat higher than the market cost. The spreads between the value investors get and the market costs are the benefits for the market makers. Banks likewise win commissions by giving liquidity to their customers' organizations.

Brokers and Banks are two significant players in the market. Brokers are commonly firms that encourage the offer of a resource for a purchaser or dealer. Banks are normally huge investment firms or financial institutions that make the liquidity in the market.

CHAPTER 18:
OPEN A TRADING ACCOUNT

What is a Trading Account?

A trading account is utilized as a way for an investor to buy stocks, comparable to investments. Be that as it may, a trading account can hold stocks, yet additionally money, securities, and many different sorts of investments. A trading account is held by a monetary foundation and oversaw by an investment dealer to run a trading strategy for the account holder. There are various kinds of trading accounts accessible, including money accounts and edge accounts.

Beginning with a Trading Account: Opening a trading account

Understand that each online brokerage account sign up process is marginally different. We should concentrate on the key components that are found in all major online brokerage firms to answer two or three of these speedy questions that we consider it. "Should I finance it from my ledger?" And the appropriate response is, "Yes," as a result of the necessities of the financier you should have any funds coming straightforwardly from your name and your name just into an account that is set up in your name and your name as it were. You can't utilize a check from a companion to fund your account. The most ideal approach to fund your account is employing a bank wire straightforwardly from your registering or investment account with your new brokerage account.

The sort of record you pick will depend upon whether your account is tax-deferred or taxable which should be something like a 401(k), IRA, Traditional, Rollover, Roth, or SEP. Is the account just for you as a person or will it have a spot with you and your partner? Which could mean it would be a joint account. Your decisions incorporate individual accounts, non-retirement, and under personal accounts you can open an individual account. Presently this ought to be nonretirement, however you should open a shared service for you and your life partner or huge other. Potentially, you may consider, opening a custodial account which would be for a minor, maybe your kids or a niece or nephew. If it won't be a nonretirement account, at that point we would be taking a look at a conventional IRA, Rollover, or perhaps a mixture like a Roth IRA or SEP which represents streamlined worker annuity plan.

Your Personal Information

As you experience the account opening procedure, your brokerage firm has to know a good arrangement of individual information about you. The information is required for account taking care of, tax tracking, and different purposes. Congress as of late passed the US Patriot Act which expects brokers to gather and confirm certain individual information. Investors are constantly required to give exact individual information about themselves. The brokerage needs this data so they can get in touch with you to examine changes in your accounts to confirm deals or buys and to tell you about an edge call.

What is required to open a Trading Account?

Online brokerage firms have arrangements concerning your privacy and how this data is taken care of. Ensure you set aside the effort to acclimate yourself with the business company's standards for the handling of your information. Coming up next is a rundown of the personal information a brokerage firm will probably gather:

Your complete name, road address, telephone number, email address, Social Security number, date of birth, US citizenship status, work environment, inexact yearly salary, total assets with or without your home, your federal tax section, and any past market experience.

Acknowledge they are required to know who they are working with and you should be direct and genuine with them. In responding to their inquiries, be certain you answer them appropriately. Many individuals don't consider how their total net Value includes their TVs and vehicles. They quite often consider their positions and accounts yet their total assets go past that. It goes into the entirety of their property and what their fairly estimated Value would be available to be purchased in the city. The equivalent is valid about the market experience; if you disclose to them you have zero market experience you might be doing yourself a damage. Recollect that if you do have mutual funds or a 401(k) or you have traded stocks previously, regardless of whether it was with another business, these sorts of trades tally towards your experience level. Erroneous data could bring about your being presented to more risk than you can deal with and in this way the loss of assets can be more noteworthy than what you can bear.

Additional Information

As consistently there is additional information the brokerage firm will likewise ask you. If you work for an enlisted broker-dealer they'll ask whether you were a director, a 10% shareholder, or policymaking official of an openly claimed organization just as which organization that may be. If you are an enlisted delegate of a business firm or a 10% or more investor in an organization, at that point you may have uncommon exposure commitments notwithstanding the data previously gave.

Deciding Your Suitability to Open a Brokerage Trading Account

Understand this information is given to decide your reasonableness to have a brokerage account. Your broker has a rule, Know Your Customer, and a brokerage firm should decide the investor's capacity to deal with risk. This is typically separated into four fundamental ideas.

1. Aggressive growth implies you're willing to face additional challenges to get additional prizes and you may wish to trade or invest in unpredictable securities.
2. The following level down is basic development that implies you need to pick up cash in the account while safeguarding the first capital however much as could reasonably be expected and you can set certain degrees of risk. "I need to do this however I would prefer not to lose over 5%," and they would close the position if it went beneath that so you could lose 5% if you pick that as your stop loss.
3. The third one is called salary and a pay risk level methods you mean to use the benefits from the account as a source of income. Trades and investments will be getting modest quantities of cash and toward the month's end, with the goal that your account balance

remains fundamentally the equivalent, anything you've made for the month comes to you.

4. The last one is the most traditionalist and that is capital preservation and this is the place the investor plans to utilize the account for just a single thing and that is to spare and ensure existing assets.

Last Steps to Opening a Trading Account

We're nearly gotten done with understanding the parameters of opening another account. The following is a normal understanding statement of what you will give to the brokerage and what the financier will give to you. You need to peruse everything that you sign and if you have any inquiries, if it's not too much trouble ask the financier preceding marking or sending any cash whatsoever.

I am of legitimate age to contract. I perceive that I have gotten, read, and consent to be bound by the terms and conditions as at present set out in the Financier Client Understanding and as amended every so often. "I RECOGNIZE THAT MY BROKERAGE DOESN'T GIVE INVESTMENT, TAX, OR LEGITIMATE COUNSEL OR SUGGESTIONS." Under penalty of perjury, I confirm

a) that my Social Security (or taxpayer ID) number appeared on this structure is right and
b) that I am not dependent upon backup retaining because
c) I am absolved from reinforcement retaining, or
d) I have not been informed by the IRS that I am dependent upon reinforcement retaining or
e) I have been informed by the IRS that I am not, at this point subject to reinforcement retaining (cross out thing 2 if it doesn't concern you).

[The Internal Revenue Service doesn't require your agreement to any arrangement of this account other than the certifications required to avoid backup withholding.]

I comprehend that Stadium Online will supply my name to issuers of any securities held in my accounts with the goal that I may get any significant information from them, except if I tell you in writing not to do as such.

I recognize that securities held in my Margin account might be pledged, re-pledged, hypothecated, or re-hypothecated for any sum due to Stadium Online in my account(s) or for a greater amount. I COMPREHEND THAT THIS ACCOUNT IS REPRESENTED BY A PRE-DISPUTE ASSERTION CLAUSE CONTAINED SECTION 31B OF THE STADIUM ONLINE CLIENT UNDERSTANDING.

Contingent upon the Brokerage included an Electronic mark is adequate – In different cases, the financier may have you print out the marked page and truly sign and mail into them.

In either case, you have to print out the whole archive for your accounts and keep a duplicate of any mark pages for what's to come.

Chapter 19:
SWING TRADING

S wing trading is a kind of trading style that centers on benefitting off changing patterns in value activity over generally short time allotments. Swing traders will attempt to catch rises and downswings in stock costs. Positions are regularly held for one to six days, although some may keep going up to half a month if the trade stays gainful. Dealers who swing-trade stocks discover trading openings utilizing a variety of specialized indicators to distinguish designs, pattern bearing, and potential short changes in pattern.

There are various systems you can use to swing trade stocks. A swing exchange subject to exchanging signals made using a Fibonacci retracement. The three most critical focuses on the framework used in this model join the exchange entry point (A), leave level (C), and stop-misfortune (B). Any swing trading system ought to incorporate these three key components.

The stop loss level and leave point don't need to stay at a set value level as they will be activated when a specific specialized set-up happens, and this will rely upon the sort of swing trading strategy you are utilizing. The evaluated period for this stock swing trade is around multi-week. It's essential to know about the commonplace period that swing trades unfurl over with the goal that you can adequately monitor your trades and boost the potential for your trades to be beneficial.

Five swing trading methodologies for stocks

We've abridged five swing trade methodologies underneath that you can use to distinguish trading openings and deal with your trades all the way. Apply these swing trading procedures to the stocks you're generally interested by to search for conceivable trade passage focuses. You can likewise utilize apparatuses, for example, CMC Markets' example acknowledgment scanner to assist you with distinguishing stocks that are demonstrating potential specialized trading signals.

1 – Fibonacci retracement

The Fibonacci retracement example can be utilized to assist dealers with recognizing backing and resistance levels, and in this way conceivable inversion levels on stock graphs. Stocks regularly will in general follow a specific rate inside a pattern before switching once more, and plotting even lines at the great Fibonacci ratios of 23.6%, 38.2% and 61.8% on a stock diagram can uncover potential inversion levels. Brokers regularly take a look at the half level too, although it doesn't fit the Fibonacci design, since stocks will in general opposite after remembering half of the past move.

A stock swing trader could enter a short sell position if the cost in a downtrend remembers to and skips off the 61.8% retracement level (going about as an opposition level), intending to leave the sell position at a benefit when the cost drops down to and bounces off the 23.6% Fibonacci line (going about as a help level).

2 – Support and opposition triggers

Backing and resistance lines speak to the foundation of specialized analysis and you can build a fruitful stock swing trading procedure around them.

A help level demonstrates a value level or zone on the outline underneath the present market cost where purchasing is sufficiently able to beat selling pressure. Therefore, a decrease in cost is stopped and value turns around up once more. A stock swing trader would hope to enter a paid trade on the ricochet off the helpline, putting a stop loss beneath the helpline.

Resistance is something opposite of support. It speaks to a value level or zone over the present market cost where selling weight may conquer purchasing pressure, making the value turn around down against an upturn. For this situation a swing trader could enter an auction position on the bob the obstruction level, putting a stop loss over the resistance line. A key thing to recollect with regards to joining backing and opposition into your swing trading system is that when value penetrates a help or obstruction level, they switch roles – what was at one time a help turns into an opposition, and the other way around.

3 – Channel trading

This swing trading strategy requires that you recognize a stock that is showing a solid pattern and is trading inside a channel. If you have plotted a channel around a bearish pattern on a stock outline, you would consider opening a sell position when the value skips down off the top line of the channel. When using channels to swing-exchange stocks it's basic to exchange with the example, so in this model where cost is in a downtrend, you would simply look for sell positions – aside from if esteem breaks out of the channel, moving higher and illustrating an inversion and the start of an upswing.

4 – 10-and 20-day SMA

One more of the most mainstream swing trading methods include the utilization of basic moving midpoints (SMAs). SMAs smooth out value data by computing a continually refreshing normal value which can be assumed control over a scope of explicit timeframes, or lengths. For instance, a 10-day SMA includes the everyday shutting costs throughout the previous 10 days and divides by 10 to figure another normal every day. Each normal is associated with the close to make a smooth line which assists with removing the 'clamor' on a stock graph. The length utilized (10 for this situation) can be applied to any diagram interim, from one moment to week after week. SMAs with short lengths react more quickly to esteem changes than those with longer periods.

With the 10-and 20-day SMA swing exchanging framework you apply two SMAs of these lengths to your stock chart. When the shorter SMA (10) traverses the more SMA (20) a buy signal is created as this exhibits a rise is in progress. When the shorter SMA crosses beneath the more drawn out term SMA, a sell signal is created as this sort of SMA crossover shows a downtrend.

5 – MACD crossover

The MACD crossover swing trading system gives a basic method to recognize chances to swing-trade stocks. It's one of the most mainstream swing trading indicators used to decide pattern bearing and inversions. The MACD comprises of two moving midpoints – the MACD line and sign line – and purchase and sell signals are produced when these two lines cross. If the MACD line crosses over the sign line a bullish pattern is demonstrated and you would consider entering a purchase trade. If the MACD line crosses underneath the sign line a bearish pattern is likely, recommending a sell trade. A stock swing dealer would then trust that the two lines will cross once more, making a sign for an trade the other way, before they leave the trade.

The MACD sways around a zero line and trade signals are additionally produced when the MACD crosses over the zero line (purchase signal) or underneath it (sell signal).

Chapter 20:
Day Trading Strategies

Your principle objective as a day investor is to get a potential everyday pattern and to exit in the correct second, which ought to occur preceding the end of the trading session. Notice that in some of the systems, you'll likewise utilize a volume marker to affirm our signs. Legitimate signals and patterns are probably going to happen during expanding or high trading volume.

Strategy 1: Ichimoku Kinko Hyo

The Ichimoku Kinko Hyo, otherwise called the Ichimoku Cloud, is a decent independent indicator. It plots on the diagram on the value activity and comprises of five lines. Two of the structure the Senkou Span, known as the cloud. The other line you need is the blue Kijun Sen line. This system is reasonable for each trading resource as its standards are pattern related.

Procedure rules: You'll open a trade at whatever point the cost leaves the cloud, which means that a potential pattern is most likely interfering with the ordinary flat value activity. You'll by then hold the exchange until the worth hinders on the blue Kijun Sen line or until the completion of the exchanging day.

Stop-misfortune rules: Use a stop-misfortune demand for this exchanging method. Since you anticipate a pattern, the Kijun Sen ought to follow the cost. The end second moves also, so utilize a trailing stop-loss order which follows the value action.

Spot it on relative separation with the goal that it is consistently at the order side of the Kijun Sen, at that point close a trade if the value breaks the Kijun Sen. Try not to sit tight for association with the stop-loss. The stop can be as close as conceivable to the Kijun Sen and to shield you from sharp moves against your trade.

Procedure 2: RSI and Stochastic Oscillator

Our second strategy includes the utilization of two trading indicators, the Relative Strength Index and the Stochastic Oscillator. These two indicators are generally used to get signals for overbought and oversold economic situations. In this manner, their fundamental reason will be to trade value inversions. This is a scalp day trading strategy reasonable for all trading assets.

Our objective here will be to scalp the market for insignificant value moves and to depend on a greater number of trades. This is a functioning trading procedure, which includes performing multiple tasks and great responses to open and close trades the correct second. The two indicators will happen beneath your diagram. They will have separate regions down there.

Strategy rules: We will open a trade when we get overbought/oversold signals from the two indicators. If the two markers go in the lower some parts of its area, we get a twofold oversold signal. We will expect a cost increment, which we will handle with a long trade. If the two indicators go in the upper piece of the zone, at that point we have an overbought signal. We have to respond with a short trade in this case. The trade will happen until one of the markers give us a contrary sign bolstered by a value move against us.

Stop-loss rules: Trades can be short as far as time. In this manner, stop-loss orders should be tight. It may be better if you settle on a particular stop-loss remove and tail it for each trade – 0.1% for instance. Some trading platforms may let you set this stop-loss separation of course with the opening of every trade.

Procedure 3: Post-Gap Trading with Price Action

The post-gap trading technique is reasonable for stock-based trading assets. As the strategy recommends, we will require a gap to apply our trading rules. Consequently, we will utilize money related assets that start and end the trading day. This money related assets have morning gaps between the distinctive trading sessions.

Procedure controls: The instructional meeting begins with a morning gap. At that point, in the following 30 to an hour, the trading assets will attempt to balance out from the madness brought about by the market opening. The system recommends that we see what occurs in the initial 30 to an hour and open our trading position dependent on these occasions. If the stock beginnings with a bearish gap and, at that point in the following an hour the cost satisfies the gap bullish way, at that point we will have adequate motivation to accept that the cost may keep on expanding. However, if the value keeps on diminishing, at that point possibly it will enter an average bearish pattern. The contrary standards apply if the gap is bullish. Another element of this day trading strategy is that we will continually utilize value activity rules to decide our leave focuses. We will utilize trend lines, candle patterns, outline designs and other on-graph arrangements to locate the best exit point for our trade. We will utilize the volume indicator to decide the finish of the morning insanity. This will assist us with hopping into a possible consistent pattern for the afternoon.

Stop-loss controls: A great put in for your stop-loss request will be the contrary side of the gap. If you open a bullish trade, a great submit for the stop-loss request will be underneath the lower purpose of the gap. In any case, if you open a bearish trade, the stop-loss request ought to be over the most noteworthy purpose of the gap.

Chapter 21:
Value Investing

Value investing is an investment strategy that centers on stocks that are undervalued by investors and the market at large. The stocks that value investors seek for commonly look modest contrasted with the basic income and profit from their organizations, and investors who utilize the Value investing technique trust that the stock cost will rise as more individuals come to welcome the true intrinsic value of the organization's essential business.

The more prominent the distinction between the characteristic Value and the present stock value, the greater the margin of safety is for value investors searching for investment opportunities. Since few out of every odd Value stock will turn its business around effectively, that edge of safety is significant for value investors to limit their losses when they're off-base about an organization.

What makes an incredible Value stock?

The primary defining characteristic for a value stock is that it has an economical valuation contrasted with the estimation of its benefits or its key financial measurements, for example, income, profit, or income. Nonetheless, the best Value stocks likewise have other alluring attributes that make them speaking to investors who use value investing strategies:

- Entrenched organizations with long histories of progress
- Consistent profitability
- Stable income streams, without immense measures of development however normally likewise without huge compressions in deals either
- Dividend payments, although delivering a profit isn't a prerequisite to qualify as a Value stock

Nonetheless, it's imperative to comprehend that a company with these qualities isn't an extraordinary value stock. Now and again, a stock just gives off an impression of being a good value for investors however a value trap is really. Value trap can keep on enduring offer value decays in any event, when their stocks appear to be appealing.

Understand More: How to Invest in Value Stocks

Keeping away from value traps

A value trap is a stock that looks modest yet isn't. Several circumstances regularly produce value traps that value investors should look out for:

Stocks in cyclical industries like manufacturing and development frequently observe their income rise significantly during blast times, possibly to see quite a bit of those earnings disappear when industry conditions chill. At the point when investors see a potential bust desiring a stock, its valuation will look modest contrasted with ongoing profit - yet substantially less so once income fall during the more fragile piece of the business cycle.

Stocks in area that underscore protected innovation are inclined to become value traps. For example, if a drug organization has a high-selling treatment however is losing patent assurance for it sooner rather than later, at that point quite a bit of its benefits can vanish rapidly. The equivalent is valid for a tech organization that is the primary mover in another industry however that comes up short on the capacity to ensure itself against competition.

To avoid value traps, recollect: The eventual fate of an organization is a higher priority than its past while valuing a stock. If you center on an organization's possibilities for deals and income development in the months and years to come, you'll be bound to discover genuine value stocks.

Is value investing ideal for you?

If your essential investing objective is to keep your danger of perpetual losses to a flat out least while expanding your chances to produce positive returns, you're most likely a Value investors on a basic level. On the other hand, the individuals who want to follow the most sizzling organizations in the market regularly discover value investing downright boring, as development open doors for value organizations will in general be lukewarm, best case scenario.

Value investors must be flexible also. The Value discovering process disposes of unquestionably a greater number of stocks than it reveals, and it very well may be a highly disappointing way to invest during a positive bull market. Many stocks that you check off your purchase list during your pursuit will continue rising in an incentive in positively trending markets, regardless of the way that you viewed them as too costly to even think about beginning with. Be that as it may, the recompense comes when the buyer advertises closes, as the edge of safety from value stocks can make it a lot simpler to brave a downturn.

Chapter 22:
Mutual Fund Strategies

At the point when you invest into the stock market, you can spend many hours looking into stocks, exploring the organizations that issue them, and picking the perfect blend to balance your portfolio - or you can get a couple of mutual funds and let the reserve directors accomplish all the work for you. Given the mind-boggling number of investments to look over and the expanse of openly accessible information to plunge into, many investors pick the last course. In any case, before you begin looking at a mutual fund, it's critical to pick the store procedure that will best meet your investing objectives.

Value funds

Value investors are the stock market variant of bargain hunters. They search for stocks that are incidentally undervalued so they can purchase shares cheap and profit from their rebound, just as future additions. As a little something extra, the sorts of stocks that qualify as Value investments will in general deliver good profits, which add to the profits created by these stocks. Mutual funds that utilization this strategy ordinarily have "value" in the reserve name. To save money on charges, search for account supports that track value lists.

Growth funds

Growth investing is nearly something contrary to value investing. Instead of searching for set up, incidentally underestimated organizations, development investors search for youthful, nimble organizations that have bunches of potential to grow. Development investing is about capital additions, as these organizations will in general furrow all their money into their extension endeavors, instead of paying it out to investors as profits. If this seems like some tea, search for a mutual fund with "growth" in the reserved name. Likewise with value reserves, many development account supports exist, and picking one can chop your expenses down deep down.

Income funds

A few investors are centered around creating a progressing stream of income through their investments, commonly either by picking stocks with high-profit yields or by purchasing bonds, which make ordinary interest installments. Many salary investors are retirees searching for approaches to enhance their fixed pay. In case you're searching for a pay driven mutual fund, you can pick one that has a blend of stock and bonds investments (these are once in a while called "adjusted" reserves) and accentuates salary, or you can get a high-profit stock shared reserve and pair it with at least one bonds reserves.

Tax-efficient funds

One of the disadvantages of investing in any Mutual fund is that when the fund manager chooses to sell shares, this movement will trigger tax bills for any individual who owns shares in the fund. This is one motivation behind why index funds will, in general, outflank effectively managed funds: There's significantly less purchasing and selling in index funds, so you're less inclined to get hit with a fat capital-gains tax bill toward the year's end. Some mutual funds mean to limit the measure of taxes they produce for their shareholders by downplaying trades, staying with tax-free bonds and low-profit stocks, and keeping away from investments that are bound to prompt an expense bill. These assets frequently have the words "tax-efficient" or "tax managed" in their name.

Tax-exempt funds

Some mutual funds take the entire tax avoidance thing to the following level by picking just totally tax-free investments. These funds commonly invest in city bonds, which are constantly excluded from government personal expenses and are likewise absolved from state taxes for occupants of the bond's state. To stay away from taxes, it's imperative to pick a tax-exempt support that purchases metropolitan bonds from just your state. If you live in an express that doesn't gather annual assessments, at that point any civil bonds store will work for you. Likewise with charge effective assets, try not to put a duty excluded fund inside a 401(k) or IRA.

Market capitalization reserves

Many mutual funds center on stocks whose advertise capitalization - i.e., the absolute estimation of the organization's extraordinary shares - falls inside a specific range. At the point when investors refer to an organization's "size" or "Value," they are by and large referring to its market top. Most organizations are classed as small-cap, mid-top, or large-cap. The meanings of these classifications differ, yet by most accounts, little top organizations have a market top between $300 million and $2 billion; mid-cap organizations are Value between $2 billion and $10 billion; and enormous top organizations are Value over $10 billion. Truly, small-cap stocks mid-cap and large-cap stocks, but since little top stocks are shares of (generally) little organizations, they likewise will in general be to some degree more riskier and increasingly unpredictable. All things considered, many investors with a drawn-out purchase and-hold technique decide to concentrate on little top assets to amplify returns.

Chapter 23:
When to Buy and When to Sell

For investors, finding a stock to purchase can be one of the best times and remunerating exercises. It can likewise be quite lucrative – if you wind up purchasing a stock that increases in cost. However, when are you expected to go in and purchase shares? The following are five hints to enable you to distinguish when to buy stocks with the goal that you have a decent possibility of bringing in cash from those stocks.

At the point when a Stock Goes on Sale

With regards to shopping, customers are consistently keeping watch for a deal. Black Friday, Cyber Monday and the Christmas season are prime instances of low costs prodding unquenchable demand for items – we've all observed the huge screen TV battles on TV. Nonetheless, for reasons unknown, investors don't get so energized when stocks go at a bargain. In the stock market, a group mindset dominates, and investors will in general keep away from stocks when costs are low.

The end of 2008 and mid-2009 were times of over the top negativity, however looking back, were seasons of extraordinary open door for investors, who could have gotten many stocks at pounded costs. The timeframe after any correction or crash has generally been an incredible occasion for investors to purchase a deal costs.

If stock costs are oversold, investors can choose whether they are "on-sale" and liable to rise later on. Going to a single stock-value target isn't significant. Rather, building up a range at which you would buy a stock is progressively sensible. Investigator reports are a decent beginning stage, as are accord value targets, which are midpoints of all examiner conclusions. Most money related sites distribute these figures. Without a value target extend, investors would experience difficulty deciding when to purchase a stock.

When It Is Undervalued

There is a lot of information needed for setting up a price target run, for example, if a stock is being underestimated. Probably the most ideal approach to decide the degree of over-or undervaluation is by evaluating an organization's future possibilities for growth and benefits. A key valuation method is a limited income (DCF) analysis, which takes an organization's future anticipated incomes and afterward limits them back to the current utilizing a sensible risk factor. The total of these limited future cash flows is the hypothetical price target. Consistently, if the present stock cost is beneath this Value, at that point it is probably going to be a decent purchase.

Other valuation methods incorporate looking to a company's dividend growth and contrasting a stock's cost with income (P/E) various to that of contenders. Different measurements, including cost to deals and cost to income, can enable an investor to decide if a stock looks modest contrasted with its key rivals.

When You Have Done Your Homework

Depending on examiners' price targets or the counsel of money related bulletins is a decent beginning stage, however, incredible investors do their homework and due determination on investigating a stock. This can originate from perusing an organization's yearly report, perusing its latest news discharges, and going online to check out some of its recent introductions to investors or at industry public exhibitions. This data can be located at an organization's corporate site under its investor relations page.

When to Patiently Hold the Stock

Accepting you've done all your homework, appropriately distinguished a stock's value target, and evaluated if it is underestimated, don't anticipate seeing the stock you purchased rise in value straight away. Show restraint. It can require some investment for a stock to trade up to its actual value. Analysts who task costs throughout the following month, or even next quarter, are just speculating that the stock will rise in value rapidly.

It can take two or three years for a stock to acknowledge more like a value target extend. It would be far and away superior to think about holding a stock for three to five years – particularly if you are sure about its capacity to grow.

Chapter 24:
Long-Term and Short-Term Investments

Investing isn't normally a make easy money strategy that you can accomplish for a brief timeframe and hope to make a lot of cash. It's regularly a drawn-out procedure that requires persistence, responsibility, and resisting the urge to panic when the market changes, as it definitely will.

You may have known about long term investments and short-term investments, yet are uncertain of what they mean, what the thing that matters is, or what investment procedure is best for you. A long term investment, as a rule, offers a higher likelihood of amplifying your arrival over a 10-year time frame, as opposed to presenting to you an exceptional yield in only a couple of years. Instances of long term investment vehicles incorporate stocks and index funds.

A short-term investment is an investment you hope to hold for 3years or less, at that point sell as well as convert to money. Instances of term investments incorporate money market funds, declarations of store, and short-term bonds. While many individuals like to profit from day trading or hypothesize with day trading, it's a risky business and you ought to teach yourself and do a lot of research before you attempt short-term investing. For the vast majority, it is simpler and more secure to anticipate long term investments.

Read more about short- and long-term investments below to determine the best investment vehicle for you.

213

Long term Investments

Long term investments are vehicles that you can hope to pay off after holding them for a time of quite a while. When investing long term, you can be more aggressive because you make some more drawn out memories skyline, so you could select to invest in an aggressive mutual fund to get the highest rate of return.

You can approach long term investing by deciding the rate of return you need, at that point searching for a mutual fund that averages that rate of return over a five to 10-year period. At the point when you invest for the long-term you should not freeze when a stock's value drops and abstain from selling because the market looks terrible.

The market is cyclical and consistently recovers from drops, although it might require some investment to do as such. However, if you pull out when costs are low, you may lose a portion of the cash you at first invested. It helps if you abstain from viewing your portfolio often, and if there's a dunk in the market, hold on and don't pull out your cash. Let the stock costs recoup after some time.

At the point when you choose how much risk you can hold up under, remember that the more you need to invest your cash the greater the risks you can take. If you need the cash in the following barely any years, adopt an all the more monetarily traditionalist strategy to your investments and pick to invest into an increasingly secure kind of investment. Another factor in picking the sort of investment might be what you are anticipating utilizing the cash for. This may decide how much risk you feel good with while investing.

Long term investments are progressively reasonable for investors seeking put something aside for a drawn-out objective, for example, retirement or a school support. You won't gain quite a bit of an arrival if you put cash into a drawn-out investment that you intend to sell in three years, or if you need to utilize the assets for an all the more short objective, similar to an excursion.

Short-Term Investments

As the name implies, short investments are generally sold in the after holding them for a long time or less. Instances, of investment vehicles that loan themselves to a shorter investment period join stocks, mutual funds, and a couple of bonds and bonds mutual funds.

You may moreover think about short term investors being referred to as a day investors.Before getting into this sort of investing, work to understand the essentials of the stock market, be cautious about single-stock buys, and be careful that it's incredibly, hard to increase better yields than the normal rate of return of the stock market (around 7 percent) by trading short term.

Moreover, be mindful to not put the entirety of your investments into only one organization. If that organization were to go under, you would lose everything. Differentiate your risk by spreading your stock investments over a variety of investments and kinds of organizations.

It is regularly simpler to pick a couple of good mutual funds that previously spread the risk for you by buying a few distinct kinds of stock. Lastly, just invest money that you can bear to lose, not cash that needs to pay the home loan one month from now.

Finding the Right Balance

Concerning investing, it is imperative to locate the correct equalization for you and your circumstance. Before you begin investing, whether it is short- or long-term investing, you ought to have clear objectives as a primary concern. Regardless of whether you are generally interested in short investments, put in a safe spot a bit of your cash for long term investments. This will ensure you if you somehow happened to lose a portion of your cash due to an unexpected market crash or a terrible investment. Investing is a significant riches building tool and not something to stay away from or fear.

Different tips:

Consider utilizing a financial organizer to assist you in deciding your money related objectives and risk resistance. A financial organizer can likewise assist you with making an investment portfolio that lines up with those variables. Your financial objectives will likewise support you and your monetary organizer to decide the best strategy for your investments since when you need the cash can likewise assist you with deciding the measure of development you need in a particular time allotment. A general dependable guideline when investing is to enhance your investments, for example purchase various sorts of stocks across various divisions of the business sectors, and have a decent parity of more dangerous investments versus those that are less risky, for example, bonds or bonds reserves. If you are investing to arrive at a particular financial objective, such as paying for a kid's advanced degree or putting something aside for retirement, your investments should begin less secure with the opportunity of a better yield when you're more youthful, at that point become progressively preservationist in later years.

CHAPTER 25:
BUILDING A PROFITABLE
PORTFOLIO

Stage 1: Determining Asset Allocation

Stage 2: Achieving the Portfolio

Stage 3: Reassessing Weightings

Stage 4: Rebalancing Strategically

Stage 1: Determining Your Appropriate Asset Allocation

Discovering your financial situation and goals is the primary assignment in building a portfolio. Significant things to consider are age and how much time you need to develop your investments, just as the measure of funding to invest and future payment needs. An unmarried, 22-year-old college graduate simply starting their profession needs an alternate investment system than a 55-year-old married individual hoping to help pay for a child's education degree and retire in the next decade.

A subsequent factor to consider is your character and risk tolerance. Is it accurate to say that you will danger the potential loss of some cash for the chance of more prominent returns? Everybody might want to harvest exceptional yields a seemingly endless amount of time after a year, however, if you can't rest around evening time when your investments take a short drop, odds are the significant yields from those sorts of benefits are not worth the stress.

Explaining your present circumstance, your future requirements for capital, and your risk resilience will decide how your investments ought to be assigned among various resource classes. The chance of greater returns comes to the expense of greater risk of losses (a guideline known as the risk/bring tradeoff back). You would prefer not to wipe out the risk to such an extent to improve it for your circumstance and way of life. For instance, the youngster who won't need to rely upon their investments for money can bear to face greater challenges in the mission for exceptional yields. Then again, the individual approaching retirement needs to concentrate on ensuring their advantages and attracting pay from these benefits an assessment effective way.

Conservative vs. Aggressive Investors

For the most part, the more risk you can hold up under, the more aggressive your portfolio will be, committing a bigger segment to values and less to bonds and other fixed-salary securities. Alternately, the less risk you can expect, the more traditionalist your portfolio will be. Here are two models, one for conservative investors and one for the modestly aggressive investor.

Conservative Portfolio

The principal objective of a moderate portfolio is to ensure its value. The designation appeared above would yield current pay from the bonds, and would likewise give some drawn-out capital development potential from the interest in great values.

Stage 2: Achieving the Portfolio

When you've decided on the right asset allocation, you have to divide your capital between the suitable asset classes. On an essential level, this isn't troublesome: equities are equities, and bonds will be bonds.

In any case, you can additionally break down the different asset classes into subclasses, which likewise have various risks and potential returns. For instance, an investor may isolate the portfolio's value parcel between various modern sectors and organizations of various market capitalizations, and among household and foreign stocks. The bonds part may be assigned between those that are short-term and long term, government debt versus corporate debt, etc.

There are a few different ways you can approach picking the assets and securities to satisfy your asset designation procedure (make sure to dissect the quality and capability of every benefit you invest into):

Stock Picking – Choose stocks that fulfill the degree of risk you need to convey in the equity segment of your portfolio; segment, market top, and stock sort are components to consider. Dissect the organizations utilizing stock screeners to waitlist potential picks, at that point complete more inside and out examination on every potential buyer to decide its chances and risks going ahead. This is the most work-concentrated methods for adding securities to your portfolio, and expects you to consistently screen value changes in your property and remain current on organization and industry news.

Bonds Picking – When picking bonds, there are a few elements to consider including the coupon, development, the bonds type, and the credit rating, just as the general financing cost condition.

Mutual Funds – Mutual funds are accessible for a wide scope of benefit classes and permit you to hold stocks and bonds that are expertly looked into and picked by finance supervisors. Finance supervisors charge an expense for their administrations, which will bring down your profits. Account funds present another decision; they will in general have lower expenses since they mirror an established index and are along these lines inactively managed.

Trade Traded Brokers (ETFs) – If you lean toward not investing with mutual funds, ETFs can be a practical other option. ETFs are shared supports that trade like stocks. They're like mutual funds in that they speak to an enormous bushel of stocks, generally assembled by part, capitalization, nation, and such. In any case, they contrast in that they're not effectively managed however rather track a picked account or another basket of stocks. Since they're inactively overseen, ETFs offer cost reserve brokers over mutual funds while giving expansion. ETFs additionally spread a wide scope of advantage classes and can help balance your portfolio.

Stage 3: Reassessing Portfolio Weightings

When you have a built-up portfolio, you have to analyze and rebalance it occasionally, because adjustments in price developments may make your underlying weightings change. To survey your portfolio's real resource assignment, quantitatively classify the investments and decide their qualities' extent to the entirety.

The other factors that are probably going to change after some time are your current money related circumstance, future needs, and risk resilience. If these things change, you may need to alter your portfolio likewise. If your risk resilience has dropped, you may need to decrease the quantity of values held. Or then again maybe you're currently prepared to take on more serious risk and your advantage designation necessitates that a little extent of your benefits be held in progressively unpredictable little top stocks.

To rebalance, figure out which of your positions are overweighted and underweighted. For instance, say you are holding 30% of your present assets in little top values, while your advantage assignment recommends you should just have 15% of your benefits in that class. Rebalancing includes deciding the amount of this position you have to lessen and dispense to different classes.

Stage 4: Rebalancing Strategically

When you have figured out which securities you have to reduce and by how much, choose which underweighted securities you will purchase with the returns from selling the overweighted securities. To pick your securities, utilize the approaches discussed in Step 2.

While rebalancing and straightening out your portfolio, pause for a minute to consider the duty ramifications of selling assets at this specific time.

Maybe your interest in development stocks has acknowledged firmly over the previous year, yet if you somehow managed to sell the entirety of your value positions to rebalance your portfolio, you may bring about greater capital gain taxes. For this situation, it may be increasingly valuable to just not invest any new assets to that advantage class later on while proceeding to add to other resource classes. This will diminish your development stocks' weighting in your portfolio after some time without bringing about capital additions taxes.

Simultaneously, consistently think about the viewpoint of your securities. If you presume that that equivalent over-weighted development stocks are unfavorably prepared to fall, you might need to sell regardless of the expense suggestions. Investigator feelings and research reports can be valuable instruments to help check the viewpoint for your property. Also, charge loss selling is a technique you can apply to diminish charge suggestions.

Chapter 26:
OVERVIEW OF STOCK MARKET

T he term investment suggests the development of new and profitable capital as new development, new producers' durable equipment, for example, plant and gear. Inventories and human capital are remembered for the economist's analyst's meaning of investment.

The economic and financial meaning of investment are identified with one another because the investment is a piece of the reserve brokers of people which flow into the capital market either legitimately or through establishments, separated in 'new' and second-hand capital financing.

Investors as 'suppliers' and investors as 'users' of long term brokers find a meeting place in the market. In this book, however, investments will be utilized in its ' financial sense', and investment will incorporate those instruments and institutional media into which savings are set. Investments are both significant and helpful concerning present-day conditions.

A few factors that have settled on investment choices progressively significant are:

Longer future or getting ready for retirement, increasing rates of tax collection, high-interest costs, high rate of inflation, bigger salaries, and accessibility of a complex number of investment outlets.

a. Longer Life Expectancy:

Investment choices have gotten critical as individuals resign between the age of 60 and 65. Likewise, the pattern shows a longer life expectancy. The profit from employment ought to be determined in such a way that a bit is taken care of as investment brokers. Savings without anyone else don't build riches; these must be invested in such a way, that the principle and salary will be satisfactory for a greater number of retirement years.

The significance of investment choices is improved by the way that there is an expanding number of ladies are working in associations.

People will be liable for arranging their investments during their working life so that after retirement they can have a steady pay. An increase in the working population, legitimate getting ready forever range and life span have guaranteed the requirement for adjusted investments.

b. Tax assessment:

Tax assessment is one of the significant factors in any nation which presents a component of impulse in an individual's savings. There are different types of savings outlets in our nation as investments which help in cutting down the tax level. These are examined under the accessibility of investment media.

c. Loan costs:

The degree of interest costs is another angle which is vital for a sound investment plan. Interest rates change between one investment and another. These may change among risky and safe investments; they may likewise vary because of various advantage plans offered by the investments.

These viewpoints must be considered before distributing any sum in investments. A high rate of interest may not be the main factor preferring the outlet for investment. The investor needs to remember for his portfolio a few sorts of investments.

He/she should keep up a portfolio with high risk and exceptional yield just as okay and low risk. Soundness of interest is as significant as getting a high rate of interest. This book is worried about establishing that the investor is getting a value return equivalent to the risks that are taken.

d. Expansion:

Each developing economy is phased with the issue of rising costs and inflationary patterns. In India, inflation has become a persistent issue since the most recent decade. In these long stretches of rising costs, a few issues are related combined with a falling way of life. Before brokers are invested, erosion of the assets should be deliberately considered to settle on the correct selection of investments.

The investor will attempt to search for an outlet that will give him a high rate of return in the form of interest to cover any decrease because of inflation. He will likewise need to decide whether the interest or return will be continuous or there is a likelihood or irregularly.

Combined with high rates of interest, he/she should discover an outlet that will guarantee the safety of principal Other than a high rate of interest and safety of principal, an investor needs to consistently bear in mind the taxation angle. The interest earned through investments ought not unduly increment his tax collection burden. Something else, the advantage got from interest will be reduced by an increase in taxation.

e. Salary:

Investment choices have accepted significance due to the general increment in employment opportunities in India. The phases of improvement in the nation have quickened demand and various new associations and administrations have expanded.

Employments are accessible in new parts like software technology; business offices, call centers, exports, media, the travel industry, hospitality, manufacturing sector, banks, insurance, and financial administrations. The employment opportunities gave rise to increasing incomes.

More wages have increased the demand for investments to acquire more pay over their normal salary. The various roads of investments can be chosen to help the ordinary pay. Attention of financial-related assets and genuine assets has prompted the capacity and eagerness of working individuals to save and invest assets for return in their lean period prompting the significance of investments.

Along these lines, the destinations of investment are to accomplish a good rate of return, later on, decreasing danger to get a good return, liquidity in a time of crises, the safety of assets by choosing the right avenues of investments and a hedge against inflation.

Investing in the stock trade is the main way the vast majority have of building genuine riches. The benchmark S&P 500 stock index has climbed 7.6 percent in the previous half-year, and strong economic data point to vigorous income for organizations.

The correct stock investments:

1. Keep pace with inflation.

2. Reach your financial goals with the correct blend of investments.
3. Reduce investing risk with a strong assets allocation strategy.
4. Reduce risk with a very much arranged technique for purchasing and selling stocks.
5. Use dollar-cost averaging to remain in the market when stock valuations are high.
6. Aren't affected by high-frequency trading.

If you are apprehensive about getting into the market, consider these six reasons you should change your reasoning.

12 Things You Need to Know Before Investing in Stocks

1: Investing in stocks is one of the many alternatives for investing your cash.

It's quite difficult to abstain from finding out about the stock market somehow. News about the stock market appears on basically every news report you hear on the radio or TV. In any case, because the paper and the financial media talk relentlessly about stock investing doesn't mean it's the best way to invest your money. It's just one choice.

One could just keep their cash in a savings account, earning a low return with very low risk. One could invest in brokers or bonds or collectibles or precious metals or foreign currency. These things have some degree of risk included, offer some degree of return, and have shifting degrees of (liquidity implies that it is so natural to sell a thing once you own it). You can even invest in yourself, improving your future income potential.

Never become tied up with the possibility that stocks are what you should invest in. They're only one option that happens to change enough constantly that it creates news. Many different investments are progressively steady and calm, which means they aren't discussed so a lot.

2: Investing in stocks accompanies considerable risk, particularly for the time being.

If you tune in to the news consistently, you'll without a doubt hear of different numbers like the S&P 500 and the Dow Jones Industrial Average going all over some sum. Possibly it went up 1% today or down 0.5% yesterday.

That is a great deal of all over development. You can undoubtedly gain – or lose – as much in a single day on your investment as you would gain in a whole year if that cash were in something steady and secure like a savings account.

Another issue is that you can have periods where there are undeniably more down days than there are up days. The last part of 2008 is where that happened and the stock market dropped about 40% that year (contingent upon how you measure it). If you had $10,000 in the stock market toward the beginning of 2008, it was Value about $6,000 toward the end.

Things being what they are, the reason would you ever invest in stocks? As time goes on – over 10 years – the stock market will in general develop at a rate of about 7% every year. It takes a great deal of years to move toward that average, however. Now and again, it'll be higher; in some cases, it'll be lower.

It is anything but an assurance, however. That is exactly what has happened generally and, later on, that pattern should proceed as long as individuals continue being progressively beneficial and creating smart thoughts. If you need a guaranteed return on your cash, you won't get a yearly return anything like that except if the economy radically changes.

The stock market makes a lot of sense over the long term. It doesn't make much for people who aren't giving a great deal of consideration for the time being. I'd state that the difference is somewhere around the ten-year mark.

3: Most individuals invest in stocks by opening an account with a brokerage – today, that is typically done online at the brokerage's website.

How precisely do you purchase stocks? Most of the time, individuals do this by opening an account with a brokerage firm. A brokerage firm is an organization that has access to the stock trade, so they'll take instructions from you, go to the stock trade, and purchase or sell stocks as per your instructions.

When you open an account with a brokerage, you typically store some cash with them by moving it from your checking or bank account. When the cash's there, you would then be able to request that the brokerage to purchase a specific measure of whatever stock you need. For instance, you should purchase $100 Value of Coca-Cola stock. You can submit more complex requests, as well; for instance, you may have a request to purchase 50 shares of Coca-Cola stock when it dips below $40 per share. Commonly, the business charges a fee for doing this.

Afterward, you may decide to purchase more shares – which means you'd submit another buy shares– or you may decide to sell your shares. In either case, the brokerage will charge you a small fee for every trade. That is how they bring in their cash. After you sell your stock, you can simply move the cashback to your savings account.

#4: Different brokerages have various qualities and shortcomings.

Normally, various brokerages have altogether different qualities and shortcomings. Some have exceptionally high fees on trades however will offer a huge amount of help to singular investors. Others may offer lower charges however be much uninvolved. Some may charge nothing for specific sorts of trades (for the most part when you're purchasing the organization's investments, which I'll clarify underneath).

What brokerage do I use? I use Vanguard. This is for the most part since I put my cash in Vanguard brokers (which I'll clarify underneath), for which they don't charge any trade fees.

#5: Investing all of your cash in the stock of a single corporation is dangerous: You can rapidly lose most (or the entirety) of your cash, however, it additionally has the potential for huge returns.

There are incalculable stories out there about investors getting in on the "ground floor" of an organization that went onto extraordinary things. For instance, if somebody had the option to purchase during the Google IPO has raked in boatloads of cash in the course of the most recent decade.

That being stated, there are a huge amount of risks here. Frequently, those immense examples of overcoming adversity avoid the way that the investors made a great deal of investments that failed before that big achievement occurred. If you make 10 investments and they're all mediocre – not procuring any profits whatsoever – and afterward make one more that wins a major return, your general return isn't that large.

While stocks can in some cases skyrocket, organizations can regularly totally fail also which makes their stock useless. Truth be told, entire industrial sectors can fall into nothingness after some time – recall, typewriter organizations were presumably wise investments a very long decade ago. You can invest in a major organization to radically reduce the opportunity of failure, yet that likewise definitely lessens the opportunity of huge achievement, as well. Coca-Cola is as consistent as a stone, yet it's not liable to rapidly twofold your cash, either.

#6: A great strategy for reducing danger is to spread out your investments over the supplies of lots of organizations, however that has entanglements, as well.

One basic strategy that individuals propose to reduce risk when investing in stocks is to invest assets into many organizations at once. If you purchase stock in 20 unique organizations in twenty distinct markets, you will reduce your danger of losing the entirety of your cash – all things considered, 20 organizations all the while falling flat is a pretty unlikely occasion. But on the other hand, you're lessening your capacity to earn big returns – all things considered, 20 organizations at the same time soaring is a far-fetched occasion, as well.

The genuine disadvantage here is that if you invest in 20 stocks, you will need to execute 20 "purchase" orders with your business, as was examined previously. If each one costs you $10, that is $200 in expenses. If you, at that point need to sell those stocks, you will need to execute twenty "sell" orders. That is going to mean another $200 in charges. If you have $10,000 to invest, that is $400 in charges that disappears directly off the bat – you're just going to get the opportunity to invest $9,800 of it (after paying the $200 in purchase expenses) and afterward they'll scratch off $200 in returns when you sell it, as well.

As such, regardless of whether you invest in an above stock, the fees will wreck those investments to average before long. You can decrease the effect of those charges by putting huge sums in a single stock, yet to that, you either must convey a great deal of risk (as your odds of losing a ton of your investments is a lot higher if you own only one stock) or have a ton of cash (with the goal that you can put sizable sums in a variety of stocks), lessening the rate effect of the expenses.

#7: Most stocks deliver your profits, which gives a stream of income to you without selling the shares.

While investors are keen on the rise and fall of the value of stocks, they're likewise extremely inspired by the profits that many stocks pay.

Profits are little installments that organizations payout to every investor, normally a limited quantity. For each portion of stock that you own in that organization, the organization will pay you some limited quantity – normally not exactly a dollar – all the time, ordinarily every quarter. Along these lines, suppose you purchased shares in an organization where the offers are $20 each. You invest $1,000 (and pay all charges yourself), so you own 50 offers. The organization at that point delivers a profit of $0.20 each quarter, which implies that at regular intervals, the organization will pay you $0.20 per share times 50 offers, or $10.

Dividends are small payments that companies payout to each stockholder, usually a small amount. For each piece of stock that you own in that organization, the organization will pay you some small quantity – normally not exactly a dollar – routinely, regularly every quarter. Along these lines, suppose you purchased shares in an organization where the offers are $20 each. You invest $1,000 (and pay all charges yourself), so you own 50 offers. The organization at that point delivers a profit of $0.20 each quarter, which implies that at regular intervals, the organization will pay you $0.20 per share times 50 offers, or $10.

That dividend cash is notwithstanding the typical value of the stock. Normally, organizations that deliver a nice dividend profit will in general have more valuable stock than organizations that never pay a dividend (however this isn't a precise principle, obviously).

Many huge investors own enough stock with the objective that they can live off of profits. Take that $20 stock. If you had $1,000,000 to invest, you could have 50,000 portions of that stock. Each quarter, if that organization pays a $0.20 dividend, you would gain $0.20 per share times 50,000 offers, which indicates $10,000. You'd gain $40,000 every year just in dividends while never selling any of your stock.

Organizations change their dividends normally. They here and there cut their dividends – implying that they're going to deliver out a smaller dividend per share this time than they did last time – and here and there raise them. They additionally now and then simply disregard them. Dividends are never an assurance, yet they are an extremely pleasant advantage, particularly with a steady organization that has a long history of keeping up and raising dividends.

Normally, the cash that's paid to you from dividends is simply saved in your account with your stockbroker, however, you can for the most part educate the stockbroker to simply send that cash straightforwardly to your checking accounts.

#8: A mutual fund is just a collection of investments, often stocks.

The term "mutual fund" is exactly what's described above. It's only a collection of investments. Regularly, a mutual fund is only a collection of various stocks; however it can incorporate different things, for example, bonds, precious metals, foreign currency, brokers, and other investments. Mutual brokers vary as far as how they're managed, with certain brokers legitimately oversaw by groups of individuals and different assets worked by insignificant individuals either utilizing extremely straightforward principles for purchasing and selling or by using computer algorithms. Mutual brokers regularly accompany charges which are typically communicated as an "expense ratio," which tells you the amount of the estimation of the fund is burned up every year to utilize the individuals running the brokers (and to procure them a bit of profit).

What precisely a mutual fund puts assets into and how it is worked is portrayed in a report called a prospectus. I'll be the first to concede that a prospectus can be a daunting (and frequently exhausting) read. One approach to get a good summary of the information in a prospectus is to visit a site like Morningstar, which assembles this information from tons of various mutual brokers.

More often than not, mutual brokers are sold legitimately by the organizations that work them. If you sign up for an account with the investments firm that deals with the particular Mutual fund that you're keen on, you can generally purchase and sell shares in that mutual fund with no expenses.

An ETF is a particular sort of mutual fund that is regularly referenced. The most ideal approach to think about an ETF is similar to a Mutual fund that itself issues shares which are then purchased and sold like some other offers on the stock market. You can purchase shares in that ETF from any brokerage. ETFs themselves are frequently a proficient method to expand, however you despite everything need to manage the "purchase" and "sell" expenses from your brokerage to invest.

#9: A file fund is a particular sort of mutual fund, yet represented by basic guidelines which implies the administration costs are exceptionally low.

Account reserves are a basic kind of mutual fund that has extremely low charges related to it. As a rule, they work by following a straightforward arrangement of rules. For instance, an account reserve may be administered by a rule that says "purchase and hold shares in any organization with an estimation of more than $1 billion." Another one may be to "purchase and hold shares that are spoken to in the S&P 500 or the Dow Jones Industrial Average."

Since the principles running index brokers are so basic, there's not a mess of cost in overseeing them, so they generally have truly low-cost pro shares. Then again, you likewise don't have individuals there settling on explicit choices about changing course if the stock market changes as the index fund just continues observing its rules.

By and large, index brokers are an extraordinary decision in case you're simply attempting to coordinate the stock market in general and have however much-assorted variety as could reasonably be expected. Index brokers are tied in with hitting the normal as intently as conceivable with as not many expenses as could reasonably be expected.

#10: I believe that, for a great many people, the smartest stock investment is index brokers.

In case you're uncertain what you're doing with regards to investing, I have a few recommendations to make. As a matter of first importance, don't invest in stocks (or some other investments) if you have any high-interest debt and you ought to get rid of it first. You ought to likewise have a healthy emergency fund. Likewise, don't invest in stocks if you have any objectives that you want to utilize that cash for in the following ten years because the short-term risk of stocks is truly critical.

Simultaneously, I would not propose investing in the stocks of individual organizations except if you can endure losing a huge portion of your cash and you have a lot of time to consistently dedicate to considering your investments. It is a risky suggestion, especially when you can't dedicate a great deal of time to continue following the subtleties of each organization that you're investing in.

This leaves you with mutual brokers, and among mutual brokers, I suggest index brokers. Instead of paying high expenses to attempt to beat the market (and frequently coming up short, in some cases because of the cash eaten by those high charges), I think that it's a superior way to deal with put your cash into index brokers and permit them to simply attempt to coordinate the market with low expenses.

You won't hit investments home slams along these lines, however, you won't lose cash quickly either and you won't need to invest all your energy researching and studying.

#11: Tax-conceded accounts, similar to your 401(k) at work, are an extraordinary alternative in case you're contributing for retirement.

Various people look at investing as a way to deal with a guarantee that they'll have a good retirement. In case that is your target with investing, you should immovably consider using your 401(k) plan at work (in conjunction with a Roth IRA).

Various organizations offer a 401(k) (or 403(b)) plan through their workplace that licenses workers to invest their pre-tax income (suggesting that you don't have to pay yearly evaluation right now on that money) into an unprecedented kind of brokerage account, next to no not exactly equivalent to the ones portrayed already. Inside that account, you'll generally have a relatively limited selection of investment decisions for the money you put in there. A couple of managers organize your responsibilities which is something you should not leave behind.

When you're retired, you can make money from that 401(k) as you wish, any way you'll have to pay income taxes on all that you pull out. Many 401(k) plans are uncommonly helpful concerning charges after withdrawal, so don't worry over it.

A Roth IRA is another retirement choice that doesn't require an approach from your employer. You can open one with practically any investment firm out there, and you put in genuine cash from your financial records – it doesn't assist you with charges at the present time, dissimilar to a 401(k). Regardless, when you withdraw money from a Roth IRA in retirement, you pay no taxes on whatever comes out of the account.

What should you invest in? For retirement accounts, I generally ask people to pick a "target retirement fund," which is a mutual fund that is included investments specifically picked to offer an unbelievable balance of good returns and low risk when your retirement date appears. Pick the one that most eagerly facilitates your ordinary retirement date and you're good to go!

#12: Taxes on stocks aren't as surprising as they would show up.

Various people worry about taxes when it comes to investing. You shouldn't stress over them.

If you invest into a 401(k), the taxes you'll pay are standard income taxes and your brokerage will help. It's basically taxed like a customary check. In case you take money from a Roth IRA, it's usually tax-free.

Envision a situation where you're putting for various destinations in an ordinary investment support. To the exclusion of everything else, you simply owe loads on your advantages and your benefits. If you get tied up with a typical store with $10,000 and later sell it for $25,000, you simply owe loads on the $15,000. In case you've guaranteed that investment for quite a while, you'll pay long stretch capital increments troubles on it – something that is resolved when you report your charges. All things considered, it's much lower than your standard evaluation rate and for certain Americans, it's 0% or 15%. Along these lines, you may simply owe 15% on the $15,000 you got, which would be a $2,250 charge. It's extremely straightforward.

Imagine a scenario in which you're investing for different objectives in an ordinary brokerage account. Above all else, you just owe taxes on your gains and your dividends. If you become tied up with a mutual fund with $10,000 and later sell it for $25,000, you just owe taxes on the $15,000. If you've claimed that investment for some time, you'll pay long term capital increases taxes on it – something that is determined when you record your taxes. By and large, it's much lower than your typical duty rate and for some Americans, it's 0% or 15%. Along these lines, you may just owe 15% on the $15,000 you picked up, which would be a $2,250 charge. It's really simple.

Profits in a typical account are routinely taxed at the lower long term capital increases tax rate – that is, if you've possessed the stock for the four months before a profit. (In case you haven't, it's taxed like normal income.) Dividends in a retirement account stay in there and you don't have to worry over taxes on them until you take money from that account.

You should simply know this: at whatever point you truly put investment money, whether or not benefits or money from selling an investment, into your checking account, you should spare some of it for taxes. I propose setting aside 20% of it, any way you may need to check with a tax capable first.

What Should You Do?

In case you're investing for the purpose of retirement, utilize your 401(k) at work or possibly a Roth IRA. I by and large enable utilizing the 401(k) if your manager offers coordinating representatives; if not, either a 401(k) or a Roth IRA is a good choice.

If you're investing just for your enjoyment, guarantee you have your accounts perfectly healthy first and acknowledge what your goal is for investing. If your goal is essentially retirement, use retirement accounts accepting there is any opportunity of this incident.

What investment would it be prudent for you to pick? I think target retirement accounts look good if you're setting something aside for retirement. If you're investing for something other than what's expected that goes before retirement, ordinary index brokers are best– just pick one based on how much risk you're willing to accept.

Reasons Stocks are Better than Brokers

Investing in stocks

Purchasing shares of stock has significant pros– and some significant cons — to recollect before you dive in.

The pros

Stocks are highly fluid. While investments money can be locked up for years in brokers, the buy or sales of public company shares can be done the moment you choose it's a great opportunity to act. Unlike brokers, it's likewise simpler to know the estimation of your investment whenever.

It's simpler to expand your investment in stocks. Hardly any individuals have the opportunity — not to mention the money — to buy enough brokers properties to cover a wide enough scope of areas or industries to have genuine diversification. With stocks, it's conceivable to build broad portfolio companies of industries at a fraction of the time and cost of claiming a diverse collection of properties. Maybe the most effortless way: Purchase shares in mutual brokers, index brokers, or trade traded brokers. These brokers purchase shares in a wide swath of organizations, which can give support investors instant diversification.

There are fewer (if any) trade fees with stocks. While you'll have to open a brokerage account to purchase and sell stocks, the value war among discount brokers has decreased stock trading expenses to $0 much of the time. Many brokers likewise offer a choice of no-transaction-fee mutual fund, index brokers, and ETFs.

You can develop your investment in tax-advantaged retirement accounts. Buying shares through a business supported retirement account like a 401(k) or through an individual retirement account can permit your investment to develop tax-deferred or even tax-exempt.

The cons

Stock prices are considerably more volatile than brokers. The prices of stocks can go all over a lot quicker than estate prices. That instability can be stomach-churning unless you take a long view on the stocks and brokers you buy for your portfolio, which means you plan to purchase and hold regardless of unpredictability.

Selling stocks may result in a capital gains tax. At the point when you sell your stocks, you may need to pay a capital gains tax. If you've held the stock for over a year, in any case, you may meet all requirements for taxes at a lower rate. Likewise, you may need to pay taxes on any stock dividends your portfolio paid out during the year. (See increasingly about taxes on stocks.)

Stocks can trigger emotional decision-making. While you can purchase and sell stocks more effectively than brokers properties, that doesn't mean you should. At the point when markets waver, investors frequently sell when a purchase and-hold strategy normally creates more greater returns. Investors should take a long view of all investments, including building a stock portfolio.

Market Timing Tips Every Investor Should Know

Study Long-Term Cycles

Think back and you'll see that positively bull markets finished in the 6th year of the Reagan organization and the eighth year of both the Clinton and Bush organizations. The Obama/Trump bull market has been going solid since 2009. These authentic analogs and cycles can mean the contrast between unrivaled returns and lost chances. Comparable long term advertises powers incorporate financing cost fluctuations, the ostensible economic cycle, and currency trends.

Watch the Calendar

Financial markets likewise crush through yearly cycles that favor various strategies at specific seasons. For instance, small caps show relative quality in the principal quarter that will in general vanish into the final quarter. Many think this is the season when the hypothesis on the New Year reawakens. In the meantime, tech stocks will in general perform well from January into late-spring and afterward mope until November or December.

The two cycles generally follow the market adage to "sell in May and go away," a strategy dependent on the accounted underperformance of stocks in the six months starting in May and enduring through October versus the November to April period.

Reaches That Set up New Trends

Markets will in general pattern higher or lower around 25 percent of the time in all holding periods and stall out in sideways trading ranges the other 75 percent of the time. A speedy audit of the month to month value example will decide how the planned investments are arranging along this pattern run hub. These value elements follow the old market insight that "the greater the move, the more extensive the base."

Build Bottom-Fishing Skills

Traders are instructed not to average down or discover falling knives. Investors advantage when building places that have fallen rigid however show qualities of bottoming out. It's an intelligent system that builds up favored normal passage and capitulation costs, purchasing tranches around the enchantment number while the instrument works through a basing design. If the floor breaks, execute an exit plan that discards the gap situation at or over the capitulation cost.

Apple Inc. (AAPL) shares bested out at $100 after a ground-breaking rally and entered a lofty remedy. Imminent investors can pull up a Fibonacci system extended over the four-year slant and recognize consonant levels that could draw in solid purchasing interest. The checked retracements bolster purchasing the principal tranche of another position when the decrease arrives at the 38.6 percent retracement at $66.

The plummet proceeded to the 50 percent level at $56, while month to month stochastic crossed the oversold level just because since 2009 and cost chose the 50-month exponential moving normal (EMA), a great long term bolster level. Investors had an additional four months to manufacture positions inside the developing base, in front of an upturn that arrived at an untouched high in 2014.

Distinguish Correlated Markets

Algorithmic cross-control between values, bonds, and monetary standards characterize the advanced market condition, with enormous rotational procedures all through related divisions on a day by day, week by week and month to month premise. This opens the portfolio to raised risk because apparently inconsequential positions might be sitting in a similar full-scale bin, getting purchased and sold together. This high connection can crush yearly returns when a "dark swan" occasion tags along.

Alleviate this risk by coupling each position with a related file or ETF, performing two investigations in any event once per month or quarter. To start with, analyze relative execution between the position and associated showcase, searching for quality that recognizes strong investments. Second, contrast connected markets with one another, searching for relative quality in the gatherings you've decided to claim. You're terminating on all chambers when the two examinations point to showcase administration.

Hold Until It's Time to Sell

In a latent strategy, investors neglect to move paying little heed to monetary, political, and ecological conditions, confiding in insights that favor long term gainfulness. What the numbers don't let you know is that they're figured with accounts that may have no relationship to your presentation. Simply ask investors who became tied up with the coal business during the time President Obama was in office. Accordingly, it bodes well for investors to distinguish a capitulation cost for each position.

Your productive investments may likewise require a leave procedure, although you at first intended to hold them forever. Consider a multi-year position that at last arrives at a noteworthy high returning somewhere in the range of five and 20 years. These grandiose value levels mark solid obstruction that can turn a market and send it lower for a considerable length of time – so it bodes well to take the benefit and apply the money to an increasingly intense long term opportunity.

6 Easy Ways to Keep up With the Stock Market

In the present condition, we have news accessible to us 24 hours every day, on TV, PCs, and presumably, in particular, cell phones.

Keeping current on significant news is more basic than any other time in recent memory, particularly if you have investments that are handily influenced by world news. The troublesome part is figuring out the entirety of the accessible news to get to the updates that are generally notable to your life.

News Websites

There are a great many news sites you can follow or buy into to remain educated. Many likewise have online existences and bulletins you can buy in to. You can pick homegrown destinations or English-language news locales from around the globe.

The most significant stories will be accounted for first. You can likewise check the locales on your PC anyplace there is a Wi-Fi association and on your 4G cell phone. Instances of destinations that offer day in and day out news inclusion are CNN, Fox News, BBC, New York Times, and the Globe and Mail.

Most destinations permit you to customize your page with the goal that you see significant classes first.

To guarantee that you get the most significant news as it occurs, you can pursue breaking news messages through most news sites. Just the news that influences individuals the most will be messaged and it will be a concise feature. If it is a report that you need more data about, you can catch up on the site for additional subtleties.

RSS Readers

RSS (Rich Site Summary or Simple Syndication) is another strategy to modify the substance that you read on the Internet. Many news destinations and financial experts give RSS channels to their substance. To peruse these, you should either download an independent peruse or utilize online peruses, for example, Feedly or Feedbin.

Destinations that give RSS channels have a standard orange and white image. At the point when you click on the image, the site gives you the connection to the channel, which you glue into your RSS peruser. The best thing about utilizing RSS is that you can total the entirety of your significant news channels, blog entries and other Internet content all on one page, to give you a preview of what's going on since you checked last.

Google Alerts

If you need to get all the reports about a specific subject paying little heed to the source, you can pursue Google cautions on Google.com. At whatever point there is another web posting about the subject you pick, Google will send you an email alert.

You can set your inclinations to get refreshes as they are found or in an everyday diary design. For instance, if you need to keep up on the progressing dry spell far and wide and its effect on nourishment costs, you can set up an alarm on the catchphrases, "dry season nourishment costs," and you will get refreshes on articles with those three words in it. You can likewise limit your alarms to specific sorts of substances, for example, pictures, videos, or news.

News Aggregators

If conglomerating and tweaking your channels utilizing RSS appears to be overwhelming, you can peruse news aggregator sites. Destinations like Google News and The Street Sleuth assemble news and money related information from everywhere throughout the web and sort out it for you. The significant advantage of these locales is that you can find new online destinations and sites that you might not have known about previously.

News Tickers

A few news sites give you the choice of downloading a program to your PC that runs a news ticker along the top or base while you are working. If you are a functioning dealer, this news channel frequently shows up on your business trading pages.

Web accountings

If you lean toward hearing your news and recent developments instead of understanding them or, for instance, if you have a long drive, you can stack up your cell phone with sound updates of breaking news and investing patterns and hear them out on your timetable.

News digital accountings can incorporate replays of meetings, reports, or they might be an every day or week after week outline of late occasions. These are normally better for longer-term investments, as the postponement between the news, accounting, discharging, downloading, and listening is well past the time assigned to make a brisk trade.

CONCLUSION

Investors and Traders have had a lot of motivation to be furious as of late. Corporate scandals. Outrageous official remuneration packages. The dot.com dive. Shameful behavior by corporate chieftains. Tainted analysis. Even outright extortion executed by trusted experts that have bankrupted organizations and robbed unwary investors of their capital. Many investors who had stacked their portfolios intensely on the equities side saw enormous parts of their retirement reserve funds dissipate in the gigantic market decrease. The pain was felt by all.

However, I accept two positive patterns have resulted from the ongoing pattern of events. To begin with, I am sure investors are progressively open to investment vehicles like options that can lessen the risk from an extreme market downturn. Furthermore, it is my significant hope that everybody involved in the market—from the active trader to the casual investor—will practice more teach and art a strong strategy before risking their hard-earned dollars. When the judicious, risk adjusting benefits of options are joined with a thorough investment plan, each investor has a strong shot at profiting in the market whether it's taking off higher than ever, declining, or trending flat.

Portraying options as a prudent market play may come as an astonishment to many people who see them as dangerous business reasonable more for high-end speculators. However, as a general rule, options can, and should, assume an indispensable role in adjusting a portfolio. They permit you to keep your risk exposure to a level you can live with, and upgrade your general rate of return. They're an astonishing device once you've figured out how to choose and apply the appropriate option techniques to meet your investment objectives.

I've been trading for more than a decade. I've been a floor trader, a trading instructor, and a market maker. I've encountered first-hand the numerous advantages options can bring to the table in business sectors. The present new innovation and moderate programming programs make options considerably more appealing as they permit each financial specialist to be outfitted with the real factors needed to make brisk, very much determined choices. These programs model the conduct of options trades for you—and give you adequate knowldege beforehand available only to the experts.

When you've grasped the utilization of options, you should likewise practice the vigilance and discipline expected to delineate a course of action and stick with it. You have to build up your own trading rules in regards to when to close positions, how much risk you are ready and willing to take, and clearly recognize what you are trying to accomplish with each trade; else, it will be exceedingly hard to benefit from trading options, or from trading other investment vehicles.

Numerous traders claim to have an arrangement, yet it's regularly only a profoundly restricted "most ideal situation" startegy. They will say: "I like Gamble and Proctor, so I purchased 1,000 shares when it was at $75. In the event that it goes to $150, I'll sell." Or—more worse yet—they may have no clue when they would truly sell—and no piece of information how high Gamble and Proctor could sensibly go for the time being. Would they sell if the stock went up to simply $98 or $125—or hang on and sit tight for a grand slam?

Alternately, imagine a scenario where that stock fals in price. Do you hold tight and, assuming this is the case, for to what extent? Without a game plan—and the order to adhere to it—you're treating your investment portfolio like a lottery ticket. It's fine to contribute spontaneously or a hunch, at that point kick back and trust everything goes the right way. However, it's limitlessly better to plan all outcomes, not simply the positive ones. Also, by consolidating the suitable option procedure into your strategy, you could create noteworthy picks up regardless of what course the market takes.

We're completely used to insuring our vehicles, right? When you have invested fundamentally in the equities markets without the insurance options afford, it's just to driving around with no vehicle insurance. Buying those 1,000 shares of Gamble and Proctor at $75 per share is like driving off the parcel with a new $75,000 Mercedes—and with no insurance. You have no drawback security if your stock crashes and tremendous liability exposure if your portfolio gets hurt. None of us would risk our lovely new extravagance vehicle like that—so for what reason would you do it with your hard-earned investment dollars?

Now suppose you concur with my idea of planning and dealing with your risk. You set levels at which you'd sell your Gamble and Procter if it goes up, and at what cost you'd sell out if the trade moves against you. You enter a sell stop request, which you accept will insure you against loss past a specific point, since a sell stop request teaches your dealer to sell your stock at the market cost if the stock trades at or underneath the cost you've set. Stocks regularly hole up or down, so your sell stop may not be executed until Gamble and Proctor have traded altogether lower than where you set your stop. Maybe you got vehicle insurance from an outsider on the road who may not be there when you truly need them.

Buying a put option would be a better decision. The put gives the proprietor the option to sell at a predefined cost. The put gives the trader or investor the certainty that the person in question won't suffer cataclysmic loss should a worst-case scenario play out. That certainty comes at a price, as does insurance for that Mercedes. Zero-deductible insurance is more costly than $500-deductible insurance, and in the two cases, you lose the premium paid if you don't have to utilize the insurance by any stretch of the imagination. However, when was the last time you heard somebody gripe, "Boy, I wish I would have smashed my Mercedes so that I didn't squander my money!"?

Insuring your investment ought to be as normal as insuring your vehicle and if you set aside some effort to figure out how to utilize basic option techniques, incorporating the ones illustrated in this book, you can radically improve the chances that, later on, you will be richer rather than being poorer.

Following years in the trading markets, I've encountered everything from solid vigorous markets and even downright dreadful ones. With the changing investment environments, options have continued to be a key investment choice to secure my trading—to increase my profits—and for unadulterated theory plays.

Throughout the years I've also observed the effect that computers and software programs have had on options trading. Each new enhancement for the technology side makes option trading quite easy, more exact, and expands your opportunity for continued achievement. With the advantages options offer—and the effortlessness trading software provides—options stay a fantastically ground-breaking and remunerating trading device.